By Doug Fields

Group
Loveland, Colorado
www.group.com

Group resources actually work!

This Group resource incorporates our R.E.A.L. approach to ministry. It reinforces a growing friendship with Jesus, encourages long-term learning, and results in life transformation, because it's

Relational
Leaner-to-learner interaction enhances learning and builds Christian friendships.

Experiential
What learners experience through discussion and action sticks with them up to 9 times longer than what they simply hear or read.

Applicable
The aim of Chistian education is to equip learners to be both hearers and doers of God's Word.

Learner-based
Learners understand and retain more when the learning process takes into consideration how they learn best.

Youth Leader Training on the Go
Copyright © 2006 Doug Fields

All rights reserved. No part of this book may be reproduced in any manner whatsoever without prior written permission from the publisher, except where noted in the text and in the case of brief quotations embodied in critical articles and reviews. For information, e-mail Permissions at inforights@group.com.

Visit our Web sites: **www.group.com, simplyyouthministry.com**

Credits
Editor: Kate S. Holburn
Acquisition and Audio Editor: Dave Thornton
Chief Creative Officer: Joani Schultz
Assistant Editor: Alison Imbriaco
Senior Designer: Veronica Lucas
Print Production Artist: Julia Martin
Cover Design: MattsonCreative.com
Production Manager: DeAnne Lear

Unless otherwise noted, Scripture taken from the HOLY BIBLE, NEW INTERNATIONAL VERSION®. Copyright © 1973, 1978, 1984 by International Bible Society. Used by permission of Zondervan Publishing House. All rights reserved.

Library of Congress Cataloging-in-Publication Data

Fields, Doug, 1962-
  Youth leader training on the go / by Doug Fields.
     p. cm.
  Includes index.
  ISBN-13: 978-0-7644-2821-0 (pbk. : alk. paper)
  ISBN-10: 0-7644-2821-7 (pbk. : alk. paper)
  1. Church work with youth. I. Title.
  BV4447.F546 2006
  259'.23071--dc22
                            2006016548

10 9 8 7 6 5 4 3 2   15 14 13 12 11 10 09 08 07 06
Printed in the United States of America.

DEDICATION

To Marv Ashford and John Allen

This book is dedicated to two "old" men who displayed joy in serving God through serving teenagers and offered much hope to those of us who have so much to learn.

Marv Ashford began working with high school students as part of our youth ministry team when he was 74 years old. He continued loving, ministering to, and welcoming them for almost 10 years until 2005 when God welcomed Marv into eternity. What a great youth worker!

John Allen is currently working with junior high students at Saddleback Church and is a hero to many of us as he demonstrates a depth for Jesus, a love for life, and a passion to continue to read and grow. John, you are amazing!

ACKNOWLEDGMENTS

Most books don't have just one author. Typically there are several people who speak into a book's content and assist the author in some manner. This is especially true with this book, which is a result of many hands and hearts contributing to make sure volunteers get some practical help.

As I grew in the training of my youth ministry volunteers, I realized that just talking to them about youth ministry wasn't the answer. They benefited from content that was written and recorded. Their insatiable desire to grow, learn, and be more effective is why this book is available today. I'm thankful for many friends (new and old) who kept this training idea alive. Hopefully I have remembered to thank the key players!

- The past and current **youth ministry volunteers** at Saddleback Church, whom I have had the privilege to encourage and train since 1992. I sure love you, and I'm thankful for your ministry-minded hearts!
- **Dave Thornton** at Group Publishing, who helped inspire the idea for this book, kept pushing me, extended grace on deadlines, and is just an all-around nice guy.
- **Dennis Beckner**, who transcribed many of my volunteer trainings and then helped me think through the content of this book and added some great insight. You have been a loyal friend.
- **Matt McGill**, who read every word of this book, challenged my thinking, poured in his insight, and treated this book project as if it were his very own. The youth ministry world will never know how significant you are to much of what I write. I'm so blessed to have a ministry partner and friend like you.
- **Linda Kaye**, my longtime assistant, who has officially "retired" but always comes to my aid to type, proofread, and pray. You're the best, LK!
- **Kate Holburn**, who has done a great job editing my lengthy sentences and clumsy thoughts into something that makes sense. Thanks for believing in and caring about this project.
- **Jana Sarti** and **Ryanne Witt**, who didn't read one word or do a thing for this book (smile) but were always protecting me and helping me find time to write and encourage youth workers.
- My family: **Cathy, Torie, Cody,** and **Cassie**…the only way I can write is because you are so sharing with your husband and dad. As you know, there is no book or project in the world that is more valuable than our times together. I love you so much!
- Finally, **Katie Edwards**, who really needs special recognition because of all she contributed. At the eleventh hour, when I didn't think I could finish this project, Katie stepped in and added her youth ministry voice throughout the book. She is responsible for all the practical ideas in the "Try It" sections. She always worked with a smile, always had a great idea, and was always encouraging. Thanks, friend! (See Katie's bio below.)

Katie Edwards has served in student ministry for more than 14 years. She has a passion for enabling volunteers to be excited and fulfilled in their ministry and is dedicated to equipping, encouraging, and empowering them to minister effectively. Katie lives in Southern California with her husband, Ron, and their daughter, Abby Jane.

TABLE OF CONTENTS

Introduction 6

52 WEEKS OF YOUTH LEADER TRAINING ON THE GO

Essentials of a Healthy Volunteer
- ☐ 1. Like Students, Love God 9
- ☐ 2. Be Instead of Do 11
- ☐ 3. Take Time to Recharge 13
- ☐ 4. Discover What You're Passionate About 15

Working as a Team
- ☐ 5. Be a Team Player, Not a Lone Ranger 17
- ☐ 6. Recruit for the Team 19
- ☐ 7. Identify Needs...Offer Your Strengths 21
- ☐ 8. Create Ministry Buzz (of the positive kind) 23
- ☐ 9. Raise the Bar 25

Leaders Are Learners
- ☐ 10. Learn Early 27
- ☐ 11. Learn From Parents 29
- ☐ 12. Learn From Other Leaders 31
- ☐ 13. Learn From Resources 33

Ministry in a Busy Life
- ☐ 14. Admit It—You Have Limitations 35
- ☐ 15. Manage Your Priorities and Time 37
- ☐ 16. Make the Most of Time With Students 39
- ☐ 17. Be Wise With Your Time 41
- ☐ 18. Use Time as a Tool 43

Tough Stuff in Youth Ministry
- ☐ 19. Use Wise Discipline 45
- ☐ 20. Be a Leader Before Being a Friend 47
- ☐ 21. Examine Your Ministry 49
- ☐ 22. Learn Predictable Behavior 51

Relational Youth Ministry
- ☐ 23. Share Life 53
- ☐ 24. Give Right Attention and Affection 55
- ☐ 25. Ask Good Questions 57
- ☐ 26. Celebrate the Milestones 59

Supporting the Ministry
- ☐ 27. Dealing With Conflict 61
- ☐ 28. Guide Good Perception 63
- ☐ 29. Live Up to Responsibility 65
- ☐ 30. Understand Your Supporting Role 67

Shepherding Students
- ☐ 31. Shepherd Students 69
- ☐ 32. Mold Students 71
- ☐ 33. Help Students Follow Christ 73
- ☐ 34. Know It's OK to Say, "I Don't Know" 75

Care and Counseling
- ☐ 35. Listen Well 77
- ☐ 36. Counsel Students 79
- ☐ 37. Be Discreet 81
- ☐ 38. Recognize Patterns 83
- ☐ 39. Help Students Deal With Grief 85

Family-Friendly Youth Ministry
- ☐ 40. Respect Parents' Time 87
- ☐ 41. Don't Drain the Wallet 89
- ☐ 42. Get to Know Your Students' Parent(s) 91
- ☐ 43. Be Available 93
- ☐ 44. Be Family-Friendly 95

Understanding Youth Culture
- ☐ 45. Learn From Youth Culture 97
- ☐ 46. Point to Christ in Culture 99
- ☐ 47. Recognize Their Realities 101
- ☐ 48. Define the Culture of Your Ministry 103

Don't Give Up
- ☐ 49. Stay in It for the Long Haul 105
- ☐ 50. Set the Pace 107
- ☐ 51. Mature in Ministry 109
- ☐ 52. Step Down Graciously 111

Theme Index 113
Scripture Index 114
E-couragements 115

INTRODUCTION

> "A large part of the lead youth worker's job is making sure volunteers have everything they need to win with their students."

You've got a youth ministry, and you've got volunteers. I know you can lead a youth ministry, but I also know you can't lead a good youth ministry by yourself. A youth ministry can only be healthy when volunteer leaders are equipped, trained, and encouraged to continue to grow and become more effective. That means a large part of the lead youth worker's job is making sure volunteers have everything they need to win with their students. This book is a step in that direction.

Volunteers who are equipped to love students and guide them closer to God serve as the backbone of a vibrant and healthy youth ministry. And as intuitive as it may seem, there is more to training and equipping youth ministry volunteers than simply saying, "Get out there and love some teenagers!"

Honestly, I don't pretend to have mastered the training of youth ministry volunteers, but I've been doing it long enough to know that volunteers thrive when they receive consistent and caring doses of encouragement, practical ideas, skill training, and tips and insights into how to be more effective.

But let's be honest: Who has time to create a volunteer training program? As a full time youth pastor, I don't have the time. You probably don't either. A lot of my past trainings have been nothing more than a scramble (usually last minute) to slap something together so I could give my volunteers "something." Typically, I'm working hard just to e-mail them occasionally, pray for them, and tell them they're doing a great job. While these are all important actions, they're not enough.

> "A lot of my past trainings have been nothing more than a scramble (usually last minute) to slap something together so I could give my volunteers 'something.'"

Youth ministry volunteers need more focused, intentional training. That's why my youth ministry friends "forced" me to put some of my training ideas into print and audio form. Now that it's done, I'm glad I did it, and I really hope you find these ideas helpful!

Youth Leader Training on the Go contains 52 training "sessions" you can photocopy for your volunteers. The handouts are written to encourage your volunteers, help them strengthen their crucial ministry, and empower them to be more effective players on your youth ministry team. Basically, these handouts are a positive shot in the arm of training that isn't cumbersome, boring, or irrelevant. There is just enough training to get volunteers thinking but not so much that they'll be dreading the next one. I know your volunteers are busy and don't have a ton of time to attend youth ministry seminars, but I also know they want help. That's why the book is called training on the go.

> "There is just enough training to get volunteers thinking but not so much that they'll be dreading the next one."

Let's see if I can anticipate some of your questions:

How do I distribute the training sessions?

Since there are 52 training sessions, you can use one a week for an entire year. If you give volunteers one session a month, this resource will last four years. It'll last 13 years if you hand them out once a

INTRODUCTION

quarter. (OK, I realize that's stretching it a little. Basically, the book is flexible, and you can do what you want!)

I'm convinced that ministry leaders like you appreciate resources that are flexible and can be used in a variety of ways. There is no one way to use this resource; distribute handouts during a volunteer meeting, send them home with volunteers after youth group, mail them, set out copies at the church, stick them to windshields, read them as a team, e-mail them as PDFs...whatever! Really, the choice is all yours.

> "I'm convinced that ministry leaders like you appreciate resources that are flexible and can be used in a variety of ways."

Should I use the training sessions in any particular order?

NO! How's that for flexibility? Use them however you want; they don't build on one another. I've put a check box ❑ by each training session in the Table of Contents. Each time you use one, check it off and date it so you can keep track of which ones you've shared with your volunteers and which ones you haven't.

As I wrote these training pages, I focused on 12 big-picture themes (for example, teamwork, families, and being a spiritual leader), which you'll see in the Table of Contents along with the 52 training sessions. I focused on 12 themes because I believe in repetition when it comes to training, and I like to find ways to say similar things in different words. If my categories help you, great! If not, use the training sessions however you want.

When I'm asked to give suggested uses for the handouts, I answer with two main options (one being a personal favorite).

- Pick a theme from the Table of Contents and send sessions from that theme during the month.
- Send one idea from each section on a monthly basis. (This is what I intend to do—12 trainings a year are good supplements to what you and I already do with our teams.)

What's the deal with the CD-ROM?

You have a choice of copying the pages and giving the sessions to your volunteers in paper form or sending them out electronically. The CD-ROM in the cover contains all 52 training sessions in PDF files. (Most computers can open PDF files with a free program called Acrobat Reader, which is available from www.adobe.com.)

The CD-ROM also includes 12 e-mail messages (we call them e-couragements). These messages are Word documents so that you can customize them for your volunteers. It's simple; copy and paste our content, add your own twist, and send your e-mail e-couragements to inspire your volunteers. Here's a quick glance at the 12 e-couragements on the CD-ROM:

1. You're Human
2. Listen
3. Investment
4. Relationships That Matter
5. Fill Your Brain
6. Ministry Is Messy
7. Lead First
8. Tending the Flock
9. They Left You in Charge...Now What?
10. Love God—Enough Said
11. You're Not Alone
12. Speak Intentionally

INTRODUCTION

Wait! There's an Audio CD, too? What's that all about?

You'll find an audio CD in the cover of this book with 12 audio training sessions. You have our permission to copy these audio training sessions and burn them to CDs or send them as MP3 files for your volunteers to listen to.

Your volunteers can listen to a training as they drive to church or small group, on the way home, or on the way to work or to a coffee shop…wherever. The five-to-six-minute audio training sessions serve as another forum for training within the big-picture themes of the written portions.

We know your volunteers are on the go, so we've worked hard to help you send training along with them. Here's a quick glance at the 12 audio training sessions on your CD (written and recorded by me, Doug Fields).

1. A Healthy Volunteer
2. Asking Good Questions
3. Being Relational: Part 1
4. Being Relational: Part 2
5. Commit to Learn
6. Conflict Resolution
7. Discipline as Discipleship
8. Shepherding Students
9. Small Group Leadership
10. Spiritual Leadership
11. Teamwork
12. The Power of Words

My prayer for you is that you'll continue to look for ways to empower and inspire your volunteers to personally connect with God—and then love students from an overflow of their relationship with God.

Thanks for being the type of leader who cares enough to get training into your volunteer's hands. It's a privilege to share in this calling with you!

Blessings,

Doug Fields

Pastor to Students; Saddleback Church

Founder: Simply Youth Ministry

Overview

1. 52 training sessions you can either photocopy or send electronically using PDF files on the CD-ROM.
2. 12 e-couragements you can customize and e-mail to breathe a little encouragement into your volunteers.
3. You can pick and choose from the short audio training sessions on the attached audio CD.

LIKE STUDENTS, LOVE GOD

from Doug Fields

FOR STARTERS

What does it mean for you to love God?

How is loving God the foundation of your ministry to teenagers?

IN THE TRENCHES

Someone I admire in our youth ministry is Ellie. She works full time; she's a wife, a mom, and a grandma; and she leads an eighth-grade girls' small group. With all of the roles Ellie juggles, you'd think she would be constantly frazzled, if not completely out of her mind. But she isn't! She's a loving, gracious, wise woman who knows God deeply. Her spiritual depth radiates. When you're with her, you sense God's presence; her love for God is very evident—in her words, her smile, and her actions.

This depth benefits our youth ministry because it overflows into the eighth-grade girls and sets a standard for other youth leaders. Ellie puts God first in her life, and everyone she encounters feels it. She has enough time to fulfill all of her roles because God rules her schedule and her heart.

TRAINING on the GO

Most people believe that a good youth worker must, above all, *love* teenagers. However, as important as that is, it's not the main element in a strong ministry to teenagers. Your primary love should be for God.

Maybe this seems obvious and simple, but I'm not referring to any ordinary love here. I'm suggesting a passion-filled love for God that is evident and leaks into the lives of those around you—a genuine love for God that is so strong that students see, sense, and experience him whenever they are around you.

It's not about your perfection. It's about presence—God's presence in your life. In order for the foundation of your youth ministry to be strong, it must be built on the leaders' spiritual passion and love for God. That means you; you play a significant part in the health of that foundation.

When you're intimately connected to God regularly, that connection will become apparent in your actions, body language, attitudes, and genuine concern for people. Students are intelligent; they can discern between someone who has a textbook knowledge of God's love and someone who has an ongoing, daily personal experience with God.

A stable, long-lasting ministry requires leaders who put their spiritual development before their ministry development. This idea isn't new. Jesus clearly explained the importance of loving God: " 'Teacher, which is the greatest commandment in the Law?' Jesus replied: ' "Love the Lord your God with all your heart and with all your soul and with all your mind." This is the first and greatest commandment. And the second is like it: "Love your neighbor as yourself" ' " (Matthew 22:36-39).

Note the distinction between these two commandments. Loving the Lord your God is the greatest, and loving others as yourself is the second greatest. Reversing this order can have devastating effects on your spiritual life. Serving in ministry and loving others can even become an excuse for not falling more deeply in love with God.

Failure to see the difference between loving God (focusing on him) and loving others (doing ministry) can result in a ministry-focused life rather than a God-focused life. Please, slow down and reread that last sentence. Does the distinction make sense to you? Your service in youth ministry should never come at the expense of your personal passion and depth for God.

Many volunteers start off with a passion for God and a genuine love for students but then allow the busyness and the pace of the ministry to rob them of their spiritual depth. If you work hard to do great ministry to teenagers instead of nurturing your love for God, you'll end up in the wrong place. There's nothing wrong with hard work in ministry; it's probably motivated by a genuine concern. However, it's nowhere near as important as genuinely wanting to follow Jesus, love him, and reveal that love by loving others.

LIKE STUDENTS, LOVE GOD

CONNECT to God's Word

"He answered: ' "Love the Lord your God with all your heart and with all your soul and with all your strength and with all your mind"; and, "Love your neighbor as yourself." ' " —Luke 10:27

- How are you currently living out what's most important?
- How are you not?
- In what ways does your ministry to teenagers reflect your love for God?

Write a response and prayer to God here...

TO THE POINT

- Loving God is more important than loving your ministry.
- Rely on God's power instead of your own.
- Don't allow ministry busyness to distract you from deepening your relationship with God.
- Allow God's love to leak into every area of your ministry.

TRY IT

Grab a piece of paper and write a letter, expressing your love to God. There are no rules for writing this letter; no one will be checking your grammar or spelling. It's just you and God and an opportunity to express your love for him.

Remove distractions...Forget about your ministry tasks...Don't think about anything but God—who loves you. You are his child, his creation. Just take a moment and love him through your written words. Take a deep breath and remember that you belong to him. It doesn't matter what you write; you can write words of praise or just write the words "I love you" over and over—it's up to you.

MAKE IT PERSONAL

BE INSTEAD OF DO

from Doug Fields

FOR STARTERS

In what ways do you get ministered *to* (as opposed to ministering to others)?

What's happening in your relationship with God right now?

How did you experience God's love for you today? or express God's love to others?

IN THE TRENCHES

Lindsey was an excellent volunteer. She was consistent; she loved students; and she was really good at her role in our ministry. However, there was something missing in Lindsey. Even though she desired to succeed in ministry, she had trouble setting the "tasks" aside and letting God work in and through her. She got easily caught up in the "ministry checklist" and in focusing on what she could do. I really believe Lindsey had pure motives and wanted to serve God. But somehow ministry didn't hold the same joy and fulfillment for her as it would have if she had let go of some of the tasks and put energy toward her own soul. Ask yourself, "How are you like or unlike Lindsey?"

TRAINING on the GO

I've been in youth ministry long enough to see that the spiritual health of youth leaders deteriorates when ministry becomes too busy. The change can happen so gradually and innocently that youth leaders don't even notice it happening. But eventually their attitudes and actions begin to show signs of burnout, discontentment, pride, and hardheartedness.

The most apparent cause of spiritual deterioration is becoming so busy *doing* the work of God that they miss the importance of *being* God's person. They subtly confuse the two—doing and being. As a youth worker, *being* connected to God on a daily basis is more important than anything you can *do*. Leading a small group, attending a student's activity, hanging out with a hurting kid, ministering to a family—these are all good things. But not at the expense of being God's person.

Jesus said, "Remain in me, and I will remain in you…apart from me you can do nothing" (John 15:4-5). This image of being connected to God is the image you should be clinging to as a youth leader. A connection with God results in a healthy *being*. When this connection is valued, you'll avoid spiritual apathy and ministry burnout—two deadly "killers" of leaders.

I realize true spirituality can be seen through visible activities such as going to church, sharing openly in a small group, and having meaningful times with God. But Christian behavior doesn't always mean a person is spiritually healthy. God isn't looking for people who act righteously outwardly but aren't healthy on the inside. God is much more concerned about your *being* than your *doing*.

I've accidentally fallen into the trap of thinking God wants my sacrifice of time and my offering of hard work more than he wants my praise and my pursuit of intimacy with him. I guess you may have done this, too.

Have you ever heard or said something like:

- I can stop reading the Bible now. I have enough material for tonight's Bible study.
- I don't need to take time for prayer. We'll pray at tonight's program.
- I had a rough week at work. I'll skip church this weekend.

Your relationship with God is more than the habits of reading your Bible and praying. Depth is revealed in the process of becoming *intimate* with God. Intimacy with God sounds incredibly spiritual, but the road to intimacy runs against the grain of almost everything I *do* in youth ministry. It's more than having a quiet *time*; it's developing a quiet *life*. Intimacy doesn't happen in a day or a week; it happens during a long-term adventure with Jesus.

My prayer is that you'll pause often to check the spiritual temperature of your heart. Be sensitive to the subtle warning signs of spiritual disconnection, and be prepared to take ruthless measures to connect with God.

BE INSTEAD OF DO

CONNECT to God's Word

"Be still, and know that I am God." —Psalm 46:10

- How are you currently *doing* instead of *being*?
- In what ways can you commit to follow Psalm 46:10—and *be* God's person?

Write a response and prayer to God here...

TO THE POINT

- Consider what it means to *be* God's person rather than just *do* God's work.
- Evaluate your inner life versus your activities.
- Make it a goal to become something deeper than merely an activity director.

TRY IT

Have you ever thought about giving 10 percent of your workweek back to God? It's a biblical principle to give God a tithe (10 percent) of our finances, but what about a tithe of our time?

Consider what that might look like for you. How many hours are you awake each day? What would 10 percent of that time look like if you gave it back to God? Commit to trying it once this week. If you give 10 percent to God, do you believe that he can handle the other 90 percent?

Allow the time to be a physical reminder of your dependence on God.

Here are some ideas, but be creative with how you spend this 10 percent of your time:

- Sit in silence.
- Listen.
- Read.
- Listen to worship music.
- Sing.
- Pray on your knees.

MAKE IT PERSONAL

TAKE TIME TO RECHARGE

from Doug Fields

FOR STARTERS

How do you define rest?

How often do you take time away from your ministry responsibilities?

Are you consistent with that time away? Now...take a deep breath and relax before you read on.

IN THE TRENCHES

I started to notice that Mike, one of our key volunteer leaders, was beginning to experience a little bit of emotional slowing (aka burnout). Mike had been a small-group leader in our youth ministry for five years. I knew that he loved students and loved serving in ministry, but it seemed as if he was losing steam.

I pulled him aside one Sunday after church, looked him in the eyes, and asked some simple questions: "When was the last time you took some time off from your normal schedule and rested?" "When was the last time you spent some uninterrupted time with God?" "When was the last time you took a week away from your Sunday school teaching responsibility?" Mike was a little embarrassed and softly responded with "I don't know."

I encouraged Mike to get some time away—time to connect with God and refresh his heart. He needed that time to quietly recharge his spiritual and emotional tanks. After missing a couple weeks' worth of meetings, Mike still needed more time away. I asked him to put his ministry to students on hold for two months while he focused on recharging. He did. Today he's healthier and moving at a more realistic pace; now we have a better youth ministry volunteer in Mike.

TRAINING on the GO

Recharge. Refresh. Rest. Reflect. Renew. Rekindle. Reconnect. These words might not be a part of your vocabulary as a youth ministry leader—especially when it comes to your personal life. But if you're going to be part of a healthy youth ministry, you've got to find time to experience these seven R's.

In the midst of doing ministry, it's easy to get caught in a routine that becomes about responding to the issues of the moment. Whatever is urgent consumes time and attention, and there's always something (or someone) screaming for attention. And by always being "on," we tend to pay more attention to the issues of the *urgent* rather than the issues of the *soul*.

When we do this, we miss the God-moments because of the crisis-moments. Too much of being "on" will cause one's heart to dry up and harden to God and his ways. But when we remove ourselves from the pace of ministry (and work, relationships, and life in general), we can recognize the dryness of the heart. Occasional time away allows leaders to hear from God, be refreshed, and focus on the depth of their own heart for God.

Most youth leaders don't take breaks because they believe either they're invincible or that ministry won't get done without them. The result: volunteers who are moving too fast, allowing their passion for God to slow down. Does that describe you? Are you so busy doing ministry that you don't even really want to take the time to read this?

Imagine for a moment that you have no plans tomorrow. No work, no meetings, no small groups, no youth events—absolutely no agenda for you to fulfill. No one needs your time. What are you going to do with the day? Do you think, "Wow, nothing to do! That's perfect! I've got a lot to catch up on"? Are you someone who always has to be moving, busy, doing something? Or could you envision yourself putting everything on hold and being still before God—recharging that connection?

I understand it's not very realistic to have a lot of leisure time as a youth ministry volunteer; your life is probably packed. But commit to finding regular ways to recharge your spiritual battery—and encourage others to do the same—then everyone will win.

Call these breaks your mini-vacation. Look for time in your schedule when you can rest, be still, read, experience silence, and just sit and listen for God's Spirit to tell you something. Remember, even Jesus took breaks away from the crowd and activity (and that was as God). Jesus knew that rest and time away were essential ingredients for his ministry. It's an essential for you, too.

TAKE TIME TO RECHARGE

CONNECT to God's Word

"This is what the Sovereign Lord, the Holy One of Israel, says: 'In repentance and rest is your salvation, in quietness and trust is your strength, but you would have none of it.' You said, 'No, we will flee on horses.' Therefore you will flee! You said, 'We will ride off on swift horses.' Therefore your pursuers will be swift!" —Isaiah 30:15-16

- Describe a time you really experienced rest. How did you feel after you rested?
- What do you have a difficult time trusting God with? How does your lack of trust affect you?

Write a response and prayer to God here...

TO THE POINT

- It's about the long haul, not the quick sprints.
- To last for the long haul, you've got to learn to recharge.
- Look for times to rest, step back, slow down, or stop.

TRY IT

Take a weekend retreat—by yourself.

Tell your closest friends what you're doing and why. Ask them to pray for your renewal, and ask for suggestions on how to recharge.

Find an available location, such as a local retreat center or a friend's house (if they're out of town). Look for something quiet and away from distractions.

You don't want to overplan, but it could be helpful to think ahead and pray about where God wants to lead you during your time away. Should you bring your Bible, journal, walking shoes, some good books? Do what's good for your soul.

Here's a sample retreat agenda:

Day 1: Reflect on where you've been. Think about experiences, hurts, or ways that God has grown you.

Day 2: Take a prayer walk, spend the whole day in silence, or fast.

Day 3: Find a serene, quiet setting, and immerse yourself in God's creation. Enjoy, relax, breathe deeply, surrender, read God's Word, journal, listen, experience silence, let go, and move forward. Take time to reflect on yourself, youth ministry, and your students.

MAKE IT PERSONAL

DISCOVER WHAT YOU'RE PASSIONATE ABOUT
from Doug Fields

FOR STARTERS

What excites you most about your current ministry role?

What do you see as your personal ministry strengths? your weaknesses?

IN THE TRENCHES

Ron has been a youth ministry volunteer for over 10 years. He's done everything in our ministry; he's the type of guy who will plug himself in wherever there's a need. But after years and years of doing anything (and almost everything), he began to realize there were elements of youth ministry that triggered his passion and others that didn't (actually, some areas he even despised!).

Ron didn't love crowds, going on overnight trips, or making phone calls to students he didn't know. He *did* love teaching and spending quality time with students he knew, and he became passionate about those things. More specifically, he loved teaching students about evolution and Creation. Because of this and Ron's desire to spend more time doing what he loved, we created a new teaching role in our ministry. Now, each week Ron shows up at a different small group (as a guest leader) and conducts a Bible study and discussion on Creation.

Not only is Ron feeling more fulfilled as a volunteer, but he's also more effective because he's meeting needs that weren't being met before. Because of his passion, students and other volunteers benefit from his newfound ministry passion.

TRAINING on the GO

If you could make your youth ministry achieve three things, and you didn't have any limitations, what would they be? (Yes, try to limit them to three.) The answer to this question will identify some of your personal passions. It's not unusual for a youth worker to just go along with a youth ministry program or yearly calendar because of a sincere desire to serve. That's a great motivation, and your youth ministry needs this type of attitude. So, if that describes you, thank you. However, it'll benefit you, your youth ministry leader, and the ministry if you spend some time defining and *then* pursuing your passions.

While you may share similar interests with other people on your ministry team, God designed you with a unique personality and skills that add twists and depth to how you contribute. By paying attention to what you're passionate about, you'll discover ways to minister that will be more fulfilling to you, more effective to students, and more honoring to God.

On the surface, it might seem that the discovery of individual passions could be an action that may divide your ministry team. Actually, the opposite result usually occurs. God brings volunteers together because each has something special to offer. A healthy youth ministry team needs a variety of passions to minister to a variety of students who have a variety of needs—definitely more needs than one person can meet.

If all the youth ministry volunteers are passionate about music, your ministry may have a lot of singing but you'll most likely struggle in areas such as discipleship, outreach, and service. Singular passion leaves you with a lopsided and unhealthy ministry; while variety creates a healthy and vibrant ministry.

Once you discover your passion, you'll be released to pursue and develop your unique design—and you'll soon find yourself more focused, energized, and effective. When you understand your God-given passions, you'll see that you don't need to be at every program or feel guilty about not doing everything on the youth ministry calendar.

In some cases, discovering what you're passionate about may lead you to change your current involvements and responsibilities. So, how might you need to adjust your youth ministry activities? How could you expand your ministry into new areas and cut back on other areas? When you, and the other volunteers, are inspired by individual passion and create an orchestra of passions—wow! You'll hear some beautiful youth ministry noise.

DISCOVER WHAT YOU'RE PASSIONATE ABOUT

CONNECT to God's Word

"Now to each one the manifestation of the Spirit is given for the common good." —1 Corinthians 12:7

- What in youth ministry energizes you?
- What drains you of energy?
- How is using your gifts in ministry an act of worship?

Write a response and prayer to God here...

TO THE POINT

- Reflect on what you're passionate about.
- Dream. Imagine how you might be more effective if your passion were tapped into.
- Go through the right channels to pursue a role in youth ministry based on your passions.

TRY IT

Make three columns on a piece of paper. In one column, list the things you are most passionate about in your ministry. In the second column, list your spiritual gifts (or your best understanding of them). In the third column, list your abilities and natural talents.

Then, ask two friends (who know you well) to create the same three columns, listing what *they* believe are your passions, gifts, and abilities. Thank them, and then meet up together to compare your notes with theirs. Based on the results, talk through possible ministry opportunities with your youth pastor.

MAKE IT PERSONAL

BE A TEAM PLAYER, NOT A LONE RANGER

from Doug Fields

FOR STARTERS

What does it mean for you to do ministry in a team?

How is your ministry's leadership team healthy? In what ways do you contribute to its health?

IN THE TRENCHES

Yolanda was a volunteer for two years. Key word: *was*. She was a quiet, committed leader who really loved her ninth-grade girls. There was just one problem—she didn't agree with how our ministry was structured, and she didn't want anything to do with the youth ministry outside of working with "*her*" girls.

She didn't attend volunteer meetings, trainings, or even all-youth ministry fun events. Yolanda believed she knew what was best for her small group and wasn't in need of outside input. She was very critical of the ministry's leadership and spoke negatively about the direction of our ministry. Eventually, I spoke with Yolanda, asking her to change her attitude and actions regarding the ministry.

Unfortunately, she didn't, and I had to ask her to step down from her leadership role. On the one hand, it was a tough decision—Yolanda really did love her girls and was an outstanding shepherd to her flock of sheep. But on the other hand, it was an easy decision because teamwork isn't possible when personal agendas become more important than the common vision. How are you unlike Yolanda? (This is tougher: How might you be like her?)

TRAINING on the GO

First, who are lone-ranger volunteers? Simply put, they are people who believe that they know what's best for the ministry and that their agenda is the one to follow. Honestly, it's a lot easier to do ministry as a lone ranger. When you're on your own, you have more freedom to do things "the right way"—which is usually just another way of saying *your* way.

A healthy youth ministry is built around a team of volunteers who believe in the ministry and are willing to set their personal agendas aside for the greater good of the ministry. It's essential for a youth ministry to be led by people who want to support the ministry, actively participate in students' lives, and genuinely contribute to meeting the needs within the church.

You can be that kind of volunteer in countless ways; here are just a few ways to strengthen your team play:

Believe in the ministry vision. It's important for you to understand and believe in your ministry's unified direction. Lone rangers tend to decide for themselves what they think is best for the ministry. But team players are passionate and excited about the ministry and where it's headed. You might encounter a situation where you would do something different from the rest of the team, but by setting aside your personal agenda, you can contribute to the larger picture of what your team is accomplishing.

Support the ministry. Face it—decisions will be made that you won't agree with. But this gives you a great opportunity for personal growth. Lone rangers take this as their cue to break away from the pack and do their own thing. But team players have the opportunity to help the team succeed instead of creating divisiveness. Your opinions and thoughts as a volunteer are very important to the team; however, humble leadership, spiritual maturity, and servanthood require you to willingly step away from yourself and support the team's direction.

Know your role. Another way for you to be a team player is to understand your role in the ministry. Because your team is made up of different types of people with all kinds of passions and abilities, it's important that everyone knows what they're supposed to do. By understanding what's expected of you, you'll naturally increase your value to the team while maximizing the precious time you invest. It's OK to define new roles for yourself in the ministry, especially if you see a strong need. But go for it in a way that isn't destructive to team unity and leadership.

Actively participate. Students are hungry for attention, and caring adults (that's you) can provide a piece of what students are looking for. Lone rangers miss out on some opportunities to minister to students. Team players participate. So, when it's game time—play along. When it's singing time—sing. When it's time to toilet-paper the pastor's house—buy the toilet paper and let the students do the work (of course). Basically, be a participant instead of a chaperone. Youth leaders decrease their value when they stand in the back of the room with arms folded scanning the crowd for problem students to reprimand.

All of these actions take intentional teamwork from youth leaders. My challenge to you is to consider ways that you may have been a lone ranger and discover how you can be the ultimate team player.

BE A TEAM PLAYER, NOT A LONE RANGER

CONNECT to God's Word

"From him the whole body, joined and held together by every supporting ligament, grows and builds itself up in love, as each part does its work." —Ephesians 4:16

- Think of two other people in your ministry who enable you to minister more effectively. Thank God for those people.

- What lone-ranger moments have you had? How can you better strengthen the youth ministry?

Write a response and prayer to God here...

MAKE IT PERSONAL

TO THE POINT

- Evaluate your contribution to your ministry team.

- Understand your role on the team.

- Be quick to support others and slow to pursue a selfish agenda.

TRY IT

Suggest to your lead youth worker that your leadership team kick off the school year (or new year, new semester, or new month) with a meeting that's themed to reflect a certain sport or a favorite team. Ask if you (and another volunteer) can organize the details and help run the meeting. Arrange all the elements of a typical volunteer meeting around the "team theme." For example:

- Have everyone come in a favorite team jersey.

- Create a sports trivia game, show sports bloopers, or play a movie clip of an emotional and inspirational coach's speech.

- Distribute water bottles labeled with your youth ministry's name, logo, or purpose statement.

- Take turns giving brief, coachlike pep talks on the value of team.

- Give everyone a ministry playbook (your why-we-do-what-we-do information).

- Get everyone "off the bench," and assign specific roles.

- Have everyone set an individual and a team goal.

RECRUIT FOR THE TEAM
from Doug Fields

FOR STARTERS

Why do you think volunteers are valuable in your youth ministry?

What role do you play in inviting other volunteer leaders to serve in your ministry?

IN THE TRENCHES

One of my all-time favorite youth ministry volunteers was a man by the name of Marv, who joined our volunteer youth ministry team in his early 70s. He didn't fit the young youth worker stereotype at all; he was older than my students' grandparents. He didn't have musical skills, moved slowly, and was horrible at dodgeball. But students loved Marv; to them, he was a caring adult who led them closer to Jesus.

When Marv passed away, the people who came to his funeral included many former students who might never have been drawn closer to Jesus if we'd settled for the stereotypical youth volunteers. How can you help find your ministry's Marv? Or how are *you* the ministry's Marv?

TRAINING on the GO

The truth about your volunteer team is that the effectiveness of your ministry is limited to its capacity to care for students. The more people praying, serving, and cheering your ministry on, the deeper it will be. While all this sounds great, it's not easy.

In order to have enough people to adequately care for students, everyone must get involved in recruiting for your volunteer team (which, by the way, is not the sole responsibility of the lead youth worker). Everyone should be committed to recruiting volunteers. The more people looking for potential leaders the better.

When you consider who would make a good volunteer, I would challenge you to rethink your ideal candidate. A youth ministry tends to attract students whom volunteers can care for. For instance, if my adult youth ministry team were filled with ex-athletes, chances are good that the majority of our students would be athletes. But because everyone needs Christ, your volunteer team should reflect what you want to attract. You want variety in your volunteers to attract a variety of teenagers. Anyone who loves Jesus and students can be a useful player on your team.

In my opinion, it's an unfair stereotype that the best youth leaders are young. Actually, many of the volunteers on my team have children who have already graduated from college. Some of my best volunteers are grandparents because they have life experiences helpful for dealing with teenagers and they have more time. They know how to work with parents, and they've had more experience with pain. While painful pasts may disqualify many from ministry, I believe a painful past actually helps youth leaders. When I know a student is experiencing pain, I want to connect the student with a volunteer who has been delivered and healed from a similar situation, and that is usually an older adult. My point is that younger is not better. *Better* is better.

At some point, you might assist your lead youth worker by asking people within your church to join your volunteer team. Be ready and willing to invite some to check out serving in your ministry at any time. You might be looking for people at a Bible study, a church service, or in line for coffee after church. The thing to remember about "making the ask" is that everyone you come in contact with is a potential youth ministry volunteer. When potential volunteers are personally invited by a church peer (as opposed to the professional—that is a paid minister), the chance for accepting the invitation increases. God has the people within a church body to care for the teenagers. They're in your church, so you just have to find them. If that last sentence surprises you, ask yourself who cares about your students more: you or God? When God gives students to a ministry to care for, it's probably safe to assume that God has the caring adults to shepherd those students. You just need to be willing to help find them.

> **Caution:** When inviting people to join your volunteer team, be sure you're aware of the process of becoming a volunteer. You'll want to tell them what to do next when you find a person who expresses interest. Healthy churches have a volunteer process in place to protect students from people with impure motives. If you're not sure whether your ministry has a volunteer application process, ask your lead youth worker.

RECRUIT FOR THE TEAM

CONNECT to God's Word

" 'For my thoughts are not your thoughts, neither are your ways my ways,' declares the Lord. 'As the heavens are higher than the earth, so are my ways higher than your ways and my thoughts than your thoughts.' " —Isaiah 55:8-9

- Think back: How did God lead you to youth ministry? How do you see him leading others to serve in ministry?

- How can you be involved in recruiting volunteers to serve in youth ministry?

Write a response and prayer to God here…

TO THE POINT

- Examine what your current volunteer team has to offer.
- Consider who might be a great addition to your leadership team.
- Discover your role in the recruiting process—how can you help?

TRY IT

With your lead youth worker's approval, try hosting a youth ministry "potential volunteer week." Get everyone on the youth ministry team involved in planning it. Pray together and think about the people in your church and what might attract them to minister to teenagers. Here are more ideas.

- Let students know what you're doing and how they can help.
- List all activities with details in your church bulletin or Web site.
- Invite potential volunteers to an information dinner at a leader's house.
- Develop a "potential volunteer" brochure. Include serving opportunities, contacts, how to apply, photos of students, and the ministry vision statement.
- Pair potential volunteers with veteran volunteers. Have the veterans call potential volunteers, pray for them, take them to youth events, and introduce them to students and other volunteers.
- Make a potential volunteer video with student and volunteer testimonials, as well as scenes of needs in your ministry.

MAKE IT PERSONAL

IDENTIFY NEEDS...OFFER YOUR STRENGTHS

from Doug Fields

TRAINING on the GO

FOR STARTERS

What do you perceive as the three biggest needs in your youth ministry?

What about your students' needs? List three.

What about three personal biggies—your own needs?

IN THE TRENCHES

A couple of years ago, some of my volunteers approached me about our monthly volunteer meetings. They were happy with the training but felt some of the other aspects of the meeting could be improved. Some of their ideas revealed issues I didn't realize existed. For instance, they saw a need to make the meetings more enjoyable and encouraging for volunteers. I reluctantly agreed with their assessment (reluctantly, because it wounded me a little—sometimes truth does that).

I was happy to have the input and gladly accepted their offer to take over the planning of our volunteer meetings. While I still continue to do the training, these leaders infuse fun into each meeting; they decorate to make a boring room warmer and create an overall welcoming environment. And because these organizers also send creative reminders about the meeting by e-mail and follow up with phone calls, we've seen stronger attendance. All this because they took the initiative!

In a lot of churches, the youth ministry is small enough to be run by one person. However, no matter what size your youth ministry might be, it's important to understand how important other team members (volunteers like you) are. They are crucial players in developing health beyond just what the *lead* youth worker can manage. In short: You're essential!

I've had many volunteers tell me they felt abandoned once they made the commitment to get involved in a youth ministry. The lead youth worker was excited to have them join the team and quickly gave them a place to serve. Then the youth worker checked that task off the list and moved on to the next demand, leaving the volunteers to fend for themselves and figure out their own role. I know this can be discouraging.

Volunteers like you have the power to take the initiative and make ministry happen through your gifts. You increase the value of the ministry to the students, church, and community.

Increasing your value might require continually identifying your youth ministry's needs. And some needs may not even be known by the youth worker, but that's OK. That's why you're part of a team. When you pay close attention to your youth ministry and become personally invested in seeing lives changed, you'll begin to identify needs and then look for ways to meet them, without specific instructions.

A first step toward identifying your ministry's needs is asking questions—a lot of them. Where is the youth ministry (or youth worker) struggling? Is there a problem with organizational skills (such as event registration, messy youth room or office, outdated publicity)? Or is he or she too busy (first to arrive/last to leave, has phone calls to make, needs help planning an event/scheduling a lobotomy, and so on)? Your offer to help in any of these areas can lift a heavy burden that your youth worker may not know how to deal with.

You could also be a direct answer to prayers of desperation (most youth pastors aren't as organized as they would like to appear; I've known one for a long time—me!). I've also known a lot of youth workers who aren't prone to ask for help. Delegation can be a frightening option. And some are simply afraid to impose on others.

Whatever the reason, if you're willing and eager to help, your initiative is needed and valued (even if it hasn't been asked for). Be gentle and gracious as you offer to surround a weakness with your strength.

Here's a short list of ways you can offer help:

>Affirmation/appreciation	>Preparation for events or messages	>Team building
>Caring for parents	>Promoting events and programs	>Tech help: graphics, Web site, e-mails, audio/video, and so on
>Decorating		
>Emotional support	>Recreation	>Transportation
>Mentoring new leaders	>Relational help	>Troubleshooting
>Mentoring students	>Research	>Vision
>Planning	>Teaching	>Writing e-mails & notes

IDENTIFY NEEDS...OFFER YOUR STRENGTHS

CONNECT to God's Word

"We have different gifts, according to the grace given us. If a man's gift is prophesying, let him use it in proportion to his faith. If it is serving, let him serve; if it is teaching, let him teach; if it is encouraging, let him encourage; if it is contributing to the needs of others, let him give generously; if it is leadership, let him govern diligently; if it is showing mercy, let him do it cheerfully." —Romans 12:6-9

- Which gifts from these verses stand out to you most personally? Why?
- Thinking of your ministry to students, which of these characteristics are strong? Which are weak?

Write a response and prayer to God here...

TO THE POINT

- Observe your ministry with a critical mind, not a critical heart.
- Meet with the lead youth worker, and share observations of needs you believe you can meet.
- After permission, begin taking steps to meet the need.

TRY IT

At your next youth group meeting, set up a video camera in the corner of the room (be sure to get permission from your lead youth work first).

Without drawing attention to the camera, record every part of the meeting. For example, capture how students arrive, how they interact with other students and volunteers, how new students occupy themselves, what volunteers do, and so on.

After the meeting is over and all of the students are gone, watch the video as a leadership team. Look for needs that went unmet; you'll be surprised at what you observe. Now, put together a plan to begin meeting the needs you observed.

MAKE IT PERSONAL

CREATE MINISTRY BUZZ (OF THE POSITIVE KIND)

from Doug Fields

FOR STARTERS

What's the perception of your youth ministry from people within your church?

Personally, what kinds of things—negative or positive—do you say about your youth ministry?

IN THE TRENCHES

Diane is overflowing with positive buzz for our youth ministry. She is a small-group leader and attends all of our camps and retreats. Because Diane loves her ministry to students and enjoys serving in our ministry, she naturally talks about it to those around her.

This made a huge difference when our youth group planned to take a trip to the mountains. All the details were planned, but we were short two volunteers. Thankfully, Diane had "connections" and recruited two more volunteers to go on the trip with us. The two leaders whom Diane invited did a great job, had a great experience, and eventually became involved in our ministry—all because Diane created a positive buzz and lived out her passion for youth ministry.

TRAINING on the GO

You can help generate a positive buzz about your youth ministry in many ways. The first and simplest way is by speaking highly of other leaders, students, parents, and the ministry's overall direction. Share with others the impact your ministry is having on lives, and remind them that God is at work and doing amazing things in and through the youth ministry.

Why is this important? Because it's easy for a negative word to bring down a ministry or contribute to a negative perception. I don't mean you should hide the negative or cover up your ministry's weaknesses; I simply mean that negative comments and careless words can create damage that can take months or even years to repair.

Therefore, speaking highly of your ministry needs to be part of your ministry's culture and not an occasional event. I ask my volunteers to help create a positive perception because I want them to be vital contributors.

Regularly generating a good buzz about your ministry can only bring about encouraging results. One of the benefits is the effect it can have on potential youth ministry volunteers; it can become a very powerful recruitment tool. I'm guessing your youth ministry is one of the 99.9 percent that need more volunteer help. Right? Well, your positive voice can lead help to the team. When you continually talk about how much you love serving on the team and being a part of the "youth ministry family," others will want to be involved with it as well. Since I'm the lead youth worker and youth pastor, they expect to hear it from me. But they don't always expect to hear it from my volunteers.

Another benefit of being positive is that students will want to be involved with your ministry. Youth ministry can be intimidating for students, especially if they're new. But if they hear positive things about your ministry, they're more likely to take the risk and check it out.

Speaking highly of your ministry also encourages those who are currently involved. You communicate value when you speak well about their accomplishments, gifts, and impact on lives. Too many people hear about their weaknesses before they hear about their strengths. Affirm other youth leaders by taking the time to brag about them to everyone in your church. By speaking positively about them, you'll refuel and refresh other volunteers.

Also, your commitment to speak highly of the youth ministry will help stop gossip. If you're telling people what good things are happening (firsthand), negative gossip (hearsay) floating around the church will be replaced by the truth. A lot of gossip comes from false assumptions or misinterpretations of what people see or hear. However, if you and your teammates are committed to telling the good stories from your ministry—every chance you get—most gossip will be stopped before it has a chance to spread.

One of your many jobs as a volunteer is to create a positive buzz. When you make a commitment to get the positive word out, you'll find that ministry gets better and your team becomes more enjoyable. You'll also find your students picking up on the positive buzz and copying your behavior (and that's a good thing).

CREATE MINISTRY BUZZ (OF THE POSITIVE KIND)

CONNECT to God's Word

"May the words of my mouth and the meditation of my heart be pleasing in your sight, O Lord, my Rock and my Redeemer." —Psalm 19:14

- Spend a couple of minutes evaluating the language you use to talk about your ministry.
- What does your language communicate to others about the condition of the ministry?
- Take a moment to offer up the frustrations you have about your ministry to God. Then spend time thanking him for the positive elements of your ministry.

Write a response and prayer to God here....

TO THE POINT

- Get caught saying positive things about your ministry.
- Highlight your youth ministry or those working in the ministry through everyday conversations.
- Be on the lookout for potential leaders and students, and share positive stories.

TRY IT

Get the word out about your youth ministry. Take some time to generate positive buzz by involving your church family in the good news that's happening in your ministry.

- Send a monthly e-mail to the youth pastor or lead youth worker. Let him or her know what's happening in your specific ministry to students, explaining what you're doing with students and describing a life-changing event you've experienced. Don't just focus on numbers and activities—share stories about the great happenings with students.

- You might also ask the lead youth worker to highlight one of your students in the church bulletin or on the church Web site. Take the initiative and write it first so it can be easily edited and posted.

MAKE IT PERSONAL

RAISE THE BAR

from Doug Fields

FOR STARTERS

Where in your ministry could you be setting higher expectations? Raising the bar? Don't know what I mean? Read on.

IN THE TRENCHES

I serve alongside a small-group leader named Kasey, who is a veteran youth worker. She has been a small-group leader for five years and seems to really enjoy her role. She is dedicated, punctual, and prepared, and she knows her job description.

Sounds like a dream youth worker, right? Well, in some ways, Kasey is ideal. But Kasey has a lot more to offer than what she currently gives. She is a brilliant writer, has a passion for Scripture, and possesses a real understanding of students. But for some reason she is content with simply showing up at our midweek program, leading her small group through a study, and then going home. Sadly, she puts in the minimum effort and is semi-passionate about being a small-group leader.

Now, I don't want to turn Kasey into a workaholic and burn her out, but I'd love to see her raise the bar by exploring new areas of ministry, challenging herself in deeper ways, and taking an occasional risk within our ministry. I want her to remain as a small-group leader because she is great at it, but I also want her to move beyond what she has known for five years and open herself to exploring new territory. I don't want her busier; I want her more effective because she has so much to offer. How are you like or unlike Kasey?

TRAINING on the GO

Raise the bar is a word picture that means "improve what you do." Or put another way, it means to raise the standard of what's currently acceptable. An often-repeated saying that further defines this word picture is, "If you always do what you've always done, you'll always get what you've always got." Another is, "If you're not moving forward, you're probably moving backward."

I believe these are realities in youth ministry. You'll likely find your ministry to students heading backward if you don't occasionally raise the bar to new heights.

When I think about my volunteers caring enough to raise the bar in youth ministry, two things come to mind: (1) **identifying their passions** and (2) **identifying their energy.** For example, I need them to ask, "Am I really passionate about the areas where I'm currently serving?" Or upon evaluation, "Do I find myself involved in this way because it's where I'm needed or because I've settled for someone's expectations?" I want volunteers to discover whether they're putting their whole heart and effort into the ministry or whether they're just coasting along doing what they've always done. Improvement requires evaluation. If you truly want to raise the bar in your leadership, you need to spend time evaluating these two areas of your ministry: passion and effort.

Let's look at those two words: *passion* and *effort*. Are you *passionate* about where you serve in your youth ministry? Passion might be defined as "a powerful emotion, strong desire, or boundless enthusiasm." Does that definition describe the way you feel about your ministry? If not, then raising the bar may be easy for you. Take some time to find that *one* area of ministry that stirs up an unusual amount of emotion, desire, or enthusiasm within you. Then work to define a role that would allow you to find that "boundless enthusiasm."

If the definition of passion does describe your current ministry role, you might have a tougher job raising the bar. You may need to examine your current ministry and take a risk with a new role. For instance, if you love being involved in camps or retreats, maybe a next step would be to lead and plan your ministry's next trip instead of merely, well…participating. Think differently. So what if it's never been done that way before? Dream big. Anything is possible when you are truly passionate about something.

Now, what about *effort*? What kind of time and energy do you currently pour into your ministry role? Are you the type of volunteer who is always preparing "on the fly," or do you sit down and put 100 percent of your effort into everything you do? Raising the bar in your ministry role requires you to put in "above and beyond" effort into your ministry.

RAISE THE BAR

CONNECT to God's Word

"Blessed is the man who does not walk in the counsel of the wicked or stand in the way of sinners or sit in the seat of mockers. But his delight is in the law of the Lord, and on his law he meditates day and night. He is like a tree planted by streams of water, which yields its fruit in season and whose leaf does not wither. Whatever he does prospers." —Psalm 1:1-3

- What does it mean to delight in the law of the Lord? Do you find this idea difficult or refreshing?
- What are the streams of water in your life and ministry?
- What's keeping you planted and growing?

Write a response and prayer to God here…

TO THE POINT

- Avoid coasting in your personal ministry. What might need to change?
- Decide on a next step for your ministry to students.
- Develop a habit of setting spiritual and leadership goals.

TRY IT

Look at the chart below, and take some time to examine your relationship with God and your ministry to students.

	My spiritual growth	My youth ministry role
What am I currently doing here?		
What do I want this area of my life to look like one year from now?		
What's an immediate "next step" in this area?		
Who in my life would provide good accountability for me in this area?		
What's the biggest challenge for me in this area?		

Now it's time to make something happen! Raise the bar and take the next step in your ministry.

MAKE IT PERSONAL

LEARN EARLY

from Doug Fields

TRAINING on the GO

FOR STARTERS

Be brave and admit it: What area of youth ministry do you simply not understand?

IN THE TRENCHES

A few years ago, we started an intern program for our student ministry program. Each year, dozens of people apply to spend two years working with our ministry—learning how we reach students and help them deepen their faith. As we read through the applications, the number one quality we look for is a teachable spirit.

An assumption many people have is that we are looking for people fresh out of college. However, many of our applicants have already been youth pastors and have learned that what they really need is to… um, learn more. I love this type of humility. Our best interns have come to our internship program bruised and eager to learn how to do ministry more effectively.

Do you remember the first day of each school year when you were a kid? You had so much hope that you would start out the school year right by getting along with your teachers, making great friends, staying out of the principal's office, and studying hard for good grades. Now, today, you may look back and feel a sense of accomplishment because you met your goals—or you may feel disappointment, knowing you never came close to what you'd hoped.

Serving as a youth leader can often be the same. We begin our youth ministry "career" with high hopes of making a big difference to students. We may be nervous, but down deep we envision students flocking to us with a desire to learn the mysteries of successful Christian living. We dream of imparting wisdom and revolutionizing their lives before the end of the first month.

Well, it doesn't take long before we're humbled and we awaken to the reality that youth ministry simply doesn't work this way.

Shortly after you start working with students, you find yourself at a fork in the road. You can either become a learner or try to fake your way through. Fakers will hide their need for more training. They believe they can figure it out on their own. Fakers eventually crack under pressure, while learners tend to become stronger leaders. Learners are the ones who find a mentor, seek knowledge, and make humble attempts to increase their knowledge and impact. They make a commitment to keep learning.

As you serve in student ministry, I hope you set high expectations for what you will learn, experience, and contribute. Instead of pursuing good grades, you're now aiming to influence and mold real lives. Try to make it a goal to arrive at youth group anxious to make a difference and with an eagerness to learn. And believe me, there's something to learn every week.

Serve with the realization that you'll always have more to learn. Make it a goal to learn valuable leadership and relational skills that are unique to youth ministry. Your continuously teachable spirit will make a sizable difference in your enjoyment and the influence you can have as a student ministry leader.

As you stay open and teachable, students will see your humble heart expressed in a desire to learn, and they'll more readily accept your leadership. You'll earn the right to lead, ask tough questions, and raise the bar for students under your care.

LEARN EARLY

CONNECT to God's Word

"Instruct a wise man and he will be wiser still; teach a righteous man and he will add to his learning. The fear of the Lord is the beginning of wisdom, and knowledge of the Holy One is understanding."
—Proverbs 9:9-10

- Think of wise and effective people you know. How does this verse relate to them?
- Who can you learn from as a youth volunteer?

Write a response and prayer to God here...

TO THE POINT

- Learners become effective leaders.
- Turn past mistakes and failures into future moments for learning and successes.
- Realize that learning more is vital to becoming a healthy volunteer.

TRY IT

As a youth worker, it is so important to rub shoulders with those who have been in the trenches of youth ministry longer than you have been. Look for a youth ministry veteran you can talk to. If you don't find someone in your church, contact local churches to hunt down a veteran youth worker.

Offer to buy lunch in exchange for answers to your questions. This time will be valuable in the context of your youth ministry, and chances are you'll also pick up some life wisdom as well.

You might also find a ministry veteran in your own church to mentor you on an ongoing, monthly basis. Or if you've been in youth ministry for a while, consider mentoring a younger leader who hasn't served as long and has something to gain from you.

MAKE IT PERSONAL

LEARN FROM PARENTS

from Doug Fields

FOR STARTERS

Quick—name the first and last names of your students' parents. How many did you get right?

In what way do you involve parents in your ministry to youth?

IN THE TRENCHES

Renee is a mom of two high school students, and she's a youth ministry volunteer. She never intended to get involved with youth ministry because her growing-up years were so difficult that she didn't believe she had anything to offer. As a teenager herself, Renee struggled with an eating disorder; she spent the majority of her high school and college years battling bulimia. But with the loving support of family and friends, she eventually won her battle.

As her own kids grew up, Renee began interacting with their friends and noticed similarities in behavior between these teenagers and herself at their age. She realized that some of her daughter's friends were battling the same disorder that wounded her so many years ago. She started talking to them and building relationships with them—eventually becoming their confidante and advisor. In doing so, she helped lead them to healing and hope.

Renee shared her story with some other women in the church, and they "pushed" her my way. Now, she has an incredible ministry to students with eating disorders. Again, she didn't plan to end up in youth ministry—which actually made her the perfect candidate. How can you connect with parents who are like Renee? How are *you* like or unlike Renee?

TRAINING on the GO

Parents should be your greatest tool in youth ministry. Not only do they love their children much more than you ever could, but they know their children a lot better than you do. Parents can offer insight into family history, behavioral patterns, lifestyle details, and personality profiles.

Until you know their parents, you won't truly know your students. And if this sounds intimidating, be encouraged: It's easier to get to know parents than you might imagine. For example, if you attend a weekly youth program, just set yourself up to greet parents when they arrive to pick up their kids. Take this opportunity to ask questions, affirm their student, or let them know about an upcoming event. Making this casual connection with parents can help open the door to a relationship with them. Basically, don't be afraid of parents or view them as the enemy (they're not).

Another idea: When you call a student on the phone, don't ask for the teenager right away; instead, introduce yourself and engage in a short conversation with the parent. You may even find that your phone calls last longer with adults than with students (especially if the students are junior high boys). The parents will appreciate this gesture more than you probably imagine. I know that, as a parent of teenagers, I'm thrilled with other adults who are investing in my kids.

Also, I believe it's very important for healthy youth leaders to have an open-door policy for parents. Invite them to be a part of what's happening—whether it's a small group, a youth group night, an event, or a social time. You may have parents who do not want to be involved year-round but are willing to help from time to time—take advantage of that opening. Any interaction, even a short one, can be the foundation for building a relationship with a parent.

Commit to learn from struggling parents and families. I guarantee that parents of your students are experiencing a tough time at this very moment. There may be a conflict brewing, or they may be in the midst of a family crisis. You may have to learn from a distance, but learn just the same—by observing and listening. You may be able to talk with students in the home to find out how they feel about their situation, and other times you can benefit from talking directly with the parents. Whatever you choose to do, learning about struggling families can help you gain wisdom in caring for students.

As you commit to gaining wisdom from parents, you'll make yourself more valuable to your students and church family.

LEARN FROM PARENTS

CONNECT to God's Word

"Get wisdom, get understanding; do not forget my words or swerve from them. Do not forsake wisdom, and she will protect you; love her, and she will watch over you. Wisdom is supreme; therefore get wisdom. Though it cost all you have, get understanding." —Proverbs 4:5-7

- What does wisdom promise if you pursue *her* in your ministry to youth?
- How might your ministry be strengthened by learning from parents?

Write a response and prayer to God here...

TO THE POINT

- Make natural parent connections—look for ways to develop relationships.
- Create ways for parents to be involved in your ministry.
- Look for ways to learn from your students' parents.

TRY IT

Get together with your students' parents for dinner or coffee. Keeping the atmosphere informal and comfortable, begin a discussion that involves great questions from both you and the parents. You might ask, "How can I effectively minister to your child?" or "How do you feel about the youth ministry?" or "What are you looking for in a volunteer leader who interacts with your child?" Parents may ask you about their student or even ask each other questions. Examples: "How do I motivate a lazy teen?" "How can I get my child to come to church without a fight?" Chances are there will be more questions than time to answer them all—and you'll build lasting relationships with parents while making them feel valued. Consider making this a frequent event.

MAKE IT PERSONAL

LEARN FROM OTHER LEADERS

from Doug Fields

FOR STARTERS

In what ways are you learning from other youth ministry volunteers?

Who are two people you have learned from in ministry?

IN THE TRENCHES

Today I left a soda can on my desk, and a few minutes later, it was full of ants. To remedy the situation, I got rid of the can and scattered some ant-killer substance; within a few minutes, the ants were swarming in it and dying. Satisfied with my solution, I raced off to a meeting. When I returned, I was surprised by how many more ants had gathered and died; new ants just kept showing up to devour the mystery ant-killer substance.

Do you have the scene in your mind? OK, now imagine what the scene might look like if one of the brighter ants decided to do something about the situation. What if an ant put up some kind of ant sign: "Danger. Stay back. Eat this and die!" A simple warning would have saved the day for countless ants.

What's the moral of this random and silly illustration? First, don't allow other youth ministry leaders to ingest ant-killing substance. A better moral might be: Learn from one another and warn one another, and your youth ministry will be long-lasting and effective.

TRAINING on the GO

A healthy volunteer is always learning. If you want that to describe you, it's important to get in the habit of regularly asking yourself, "Am I learning from other leaders in ministry, or am I simply repeating others' mistakes?" Another question might be, "What lessons should I be learning from another leader?" By asking these types of questions, you'll keep learning on your radar and move along the path toward becoming an ever-better youth leader.

If there are several volunteers on your youth ministry team, you probably have tons of experiences and lessons you can share with each other. To make this kind of learning a goal, you must possess humility; a desire to learn requires being humble enough to know that you always have more to learn.

Here are a few ways you might consider helping one another to become better learners:

Learn from others' life experiences. It's valuable to share your own life experiences with the other volunteers and learn about their life experiences. Not only will knowing about one another's experiences help your ministry team, but your students can benefit from what you learn about one another, as well. For instance, imagine that a student is dealing with a tough family situation (that doesn't take much imagination, right?). If you know that another volunteer has been in a similar situation, you'll be able to direct that student to a volunteer who's able to use personal experience to relate to the student.

Learn from past mistakes. A common trap for those of us in leadership is the fear that others will see our weaknesses and failures. Though it is difficult to admit failures, it is often through the confession of our mistakes that others learn and succeed.

Leaders need to be learning from one another's mistakes and painful experiences. Don't limit your sharing to your good experiences; learning from the past (all of it) is a great way to prepare for future ministry. I've made plenty of mistakes and have seen my share of failures and hurts. But after 25-plus years of youth ministry, I become a helpful asset to other leaders when I share those painful experiences—and what I've learned from my failures and hurts. God won't waste my hurts. He'll use them to help others.

Train for the future. Get in the habit of arriving at your volunteer leader meetings with the goal of sharing with others. Ask for advice, help train others in skills you've developed, share the problems you've encountered, and make a commitment to keep sharing and growing as a team. As you support one another in your failures, you'll create an accepting environment where learning is valued. During your times together, look for opportunities to ask fellow volunteers to share about what they're learning in their ministry to students.

Learning is essential to leading. If you aren't committed to learning, you'll either continue making mistakes or miss growth opportunities. Learning from the experiences of others will maximize your ministry effectiveness and prepare you to better meet your students' needs.

LEARN FROM OTHER LEADERS

CONNECT to God's Word

"Therefore confess your sins to each other and pray for each other so that you may be healed. The prayer of a righteous man is powerful and effective." —James 5:16

- What place does confession have in learning from others?

- How are you currently learning from someone else's failures or successes?

- Which of your failures and successes will others learn from?

Write a response and prayer to God here...

TO THE POINT

- Value learning and make it part of your culture.

- Pursue humility.

- Learn from others' experiences.

TRY IT

Find a file folder, and label it "my experiences." Keep it within easy reach. On the outside of the file, make an identifiable grid of what's inside. For example, "1. personal experiences, 2. painful experiences, 3. ministry experiences, and 4. spiritual experiences." Then, every week, take some time to write on index cards key words that fit with each of these four headings. Number the index cards (1–4), and file them accordingly. Before your volunteer meetings (or when you're hanging out with youth leaders or the youth pastor), grab the file. During your time with other volunteers, share one of your current stories so others can learn from you. These experiences will enhance your ministry to students as well as help train other volunteers who are humble enough to learn.

MAKE IT PERSONAL

LEARN FROM RESOURCES

from Doug Fields

FOR STARTERS

What's the last book you read from cover to cover? What impact did it have on you?

What resources have helped make your youth ministry more effective?

IN THE TRENCHES

Andy is one of my long-term volunteers who constantly puts me to shame with his intense desire to learn. He's always commenting on a new youth ministry resource, a new Web site he's visited, or a new magazine he's found. I often tell him, "I'm the youth pastor and I should be telling you about these things." He smiles and appeases me by replying that I'm the lead youth worker but he's really the leader because he's so committed to learning. Leaders are committed learners—and Andy sets the pace.

With so much knowledge and access to resources, Andy is also very helpful to other volunteers because he directs them to the right resources. (I just wish he'd talk about my books.) How are you like or unlike Andy?

TRAINING on the GO

To be an effective volunteer, you'll need to regularly sharpen your mind, heart, and skills. Many great resources exist that'll help you become a better youth ministry leader—as youth ministry becomes a stronger and more academic pursuit, dozens of books and tools are published each year. My suggestion is to try to read at least two books or resources a year: one that'll help your own spiritual growth and one to sharpen your youth ministry skills.

Learning and growing in your own faith is an important part of being a youth ministry leader. Reading a book about building your faith may not seem, at first, a youth ministry–related topic. However, if you're going to lead teenagers closer to God, you need to be growing spiritually yourself. Teaching students out of your own growth is the most powerful way to help them develop.

Finding resources that will help with your youth ministry skills is often one of personal choice or recommendation. I know I've enjoyed books that other youth workers didn't like, and vice versa. Ask a few other youth leaders to suggest the "one" book that every youth worker should read—and then track it down.

I get almost all of my youth ministry books and resources online because I can easily find them, read excerpts and samples of the ideas, and view other people's opinions before making the purchase. Two sources for good youth ministry resources are www.simplyyouthministry.com and www.youthministry.com.

If your youth ministry or church does not already have one, help begin and build a youth ministry library. When you find a book or resource that's helpful to you, donate it to the library for others to read after you've finished with it. This will give all your leaders the opportunity to become well rounded, both personally and in their ministry to youth.

Of course, books are not the only helpful youth ministry resource available to you. The list is endless—whether the need is spiritual growth, foundational practices of youth ministry, or great ideas and activities for Bible studies, worship events, and service projects. You can find multimedia kits, complete programs, game books, CDs and DVDs, youth ministry and family-dedicated Web sites, and Internet podcasts focused on youth ministry issues.

One of the biggest myths about youth ministry is that every idea has to be original and created specifically for your ministry. Buying into this myth has wasted countless hours. The best use of your creativity is learning from resources created by others who have already been where you want to take your ministry. Using the best youth ministry tools will relieve the pressure of unrealistic expectations and, most importantly, free up your time to do relational ministry with your students.

LEARN FROM RESOURCES

CONNECT to God's Word

"Brothers, I do not consider myself yet to have taken hold of it. But one thing I do: Forgetting what is behind and straining toward what is ahead, I press on toward the goal to win the prize for which God has called me heavenward in Christ Jesus." —Philippians 3:13-14

- This verse is often understood in terms of forgetting the bad that has happened and pressing on toward the mysterious and miraculous that God can bring (specifically, eternal life because of Jesus' resurrection). What if, however, you read it through the lens of a ministry that is going well and a youth leader who is healthy? What does it mean for you then?
- How can you press on toward excellence and pursue a ministry full of continual learning?

Write a response and prayer to God here...

TO THE POINT

- Expand your mind; find resources that'll sharpen your ministry.
- Grow your youth ministry knowledge.
- Don't reinvent the wheel; take advantage of the ideas that are already available.

TRY IT

Connect with three or four youth workers. They can be from your own youth ministry setting or from another church or youth ministry organization. Invite these youth workers to a resource-sharing meeting. Have them each bring several of their favorite youth ministry resources. If the resources are free to photocopy, have each person bring enough copies for all attendees. Take time to talk about the different resources and why they are valuable. Hopefully, you'll leave the meeting with great ideas, more learning, and a few new resources. If it's helpful, reschedule for six months later and stay on the lookout for new resources to swap.

MAKE IT PERSONAL

ADMIT IT—YOU HAVE LIMITATIONS

from Doug Fields

TRAINING on the GO

FOR STARTERS

How easy or difficult is it to admit you have limitations in youth ministry?

Who knows your ministry limitations? Or who could you share them with?

IN THE TRENCHES

When I first began as a youth ministry volunteer, I felt overwhelmed by the idea that I had to do everything. Soon I became miserable because I'm not a very good administrator. Figuring out details came easy to me, but I had a more difficult time pulling them off. I needed to learn the lesson of acknowledging my limitations and humbly asking for help from within the body of Christ.

Once I did this, my life and ministry began to change. I surrounded myself with some volunteers who were very detail-oriented; they picked up my slack and allowed me to focus on my areas of strength.

They hated teaching, and I hated carrying out details. We were a fit! But it almost never came to "we" until I realized "I" couldn't do it all. If you have learned this valuable lesson, you are a highly valued volunteer. If you haven't learned this lesson, my prayer is that you'll learn it before you burn out by trying to do everything yourself. You have too much to offer your youth ministry to believe that you have to do everything.

A funny thing happened as I sat down to write: I got writer's block. The words, thoughts, and ideas weren't flowing; I couldn't figure out what I wanted to write.

The irony was that, after a few hours, it finally occurred to me that I needed to get some help (the theme of this training). So I asked a couple of my youth ministry volunteers for ideas, and they gave me some solid direction—it was so great that I was disappointed I didn't ask earlier. What follows is inspired by what they shared with me.

Many people go through life trying to be self-sufficient (what I was doing when I sat down to write this). They love the thought of doing anything they "set their minds to" and don't really think they need anyone's help. If that describes you, can I gently point out that you are missing the point of God's design for the body of Christ? God never intended for you to live life in isolation and do everything by yourself.

It took me a long time, but I finally accepted the fact that I am "better together" when my strengths and weaknesses are mixed with others who have gifts and skills that make me more effective. I want to become the type of person who has enough humility and wisdom to ask others to compensate for my limitations. What about you?

Some of the fears people struggle with when it comes to asking for help include: The credit may go to someone else; the quality of the final product may not be as good; my idea might be misunderstood or reinterpreted; or people are too busy and don't have time to help me.

Those are valid concerns, and I've shared them. But none of these fears prevents me from asking for help because the result of asking is that I'm able to spend more time in my gifted areas. My humility is strengthened when someone does a better job than I could ever do. When this happens, I'm reminded of God's design that the body of Christ works together and that my personal youth ministry can't survive on my skills alone. I need others—and so do you.

Don't be apprehensive about getting help when you need it. It's foolish to try to handle a situation you don't understand or aren't experienced with. For example, you may realize that you are not good at counseling teenagers, teaching a Bible study, or speaking in front of groups. Wherever you experience a limitation, be open to learning from others who may excel in your weaker areas. This doesn't mean you'll never master those skills. It does mean you can continue learning as you focus on the areas where you're strong.

ADMIT IT—YOU HAVE LIMITATIONS

CONNECT to God's Word

"Two are better than one, because they have a good return for their work: If one falls down, his friend can help him up. But pity the man who falls and has no one to help him up!" —Ecclesiastes 4:9-10

- When was the last time you had to ask (or should have asked) someone else for help with something you could not do on your own? How did you feel about asking?

- What does your attitude about asking for help tell you about how you view yourself?

Write a response and prayer to God here...

TO THE POINT

- Realize you don't have to do everything alone.
- Others have strengths where you are weak.
- Understand your limitations, and ask for help.

TRY IT

For your next volunteer leader meeting or team get-together, suggest that each person bring something that represents a gift or strength.

Depending on how well you know everyone, you might even assign ideas. For instance, have the great cook bring a dessert, and ask the teacher to prepare a short devotion for your time together. Or if someone has the gift of encouragement, have him or her write a personal note to each attendee.

At one point in your meeting, take a moment to highlight how different you all are and how unique each of your strengths is. As individuals we each have limitations, but as a group of people who know their strengths, we can make so much more possible. You are better together.

MAKE IT PERSONAL

MANAGE YOUR PRIORITIES AND TIME

from Doug Fields

FOR STARTERS

What's something you wish you had more time for in a typical day?

What steals your time away from those things?

IN THE TRENCHES

Christy was a single mom, had a full-time job, and was involved in our youth ministry. She was devoted to her kids and lived a balanced life. She was someone who really loved teenagers, but she had limited time to give.

She was a great volunteer, and as the youth pastor, I really wanted her to be involved because she was so good with students. I kept asking for more, and she kept rejecting me. She knew her priorities and couldn't give me the time I hoped for.

At first my pride was hurt because she continued to reject me, but ultimately (when I grew up) I realized that she was right to maintain her priorities no matter how much I begged. She was a poster child of health. Because of her priorities and her courage to not overcommit, she became a long-term and valuable volunteer. Her spiritual growth and her kids came first. And even though she did not have a lot of time to give, she made a huge impact on students and other volunteer leaders—by living a balanced, Christ-honoring life and not feeling guilty about what she couldn't do. How are you like or unlike Christy? How can she be an example to you?

TRAINING on the GO

To be a good steward of the time, talents, and responsibilities God has given you, it's vital that you figure out how to manage your time and ministry priorities. The main reason? Well, youth ministry never stops. Without any time management, you won't survive the marathon of youth ministry. You might have a strong, short sprint for a semester or a year, but you won't be around to watch students graduate. Healthy youth volunteers recognize that teenagers don't need more sprinters, and they learn how to pace themselves to become seasoned marathon runners.

The first step in managing your time is defining your priorities. What deserves your best time? Your relationship with God? Family? Think about your top priority and ask yourself, What does that time look like? Is that priority getting leftovers because your day is so full? If you don't take the time to determine what matters most in life, it's very easy for the small, menial, and often unimportant things to consume you.

Consider designing a time budget; it'll help you identify time for what's most important. In my own life, I've found it helpful to organize each day of the week into several blocks of time. Compartmentalizing my life this way helps me to be more strategic about maximizing time, streamlining my life, and giving my most energetic part of the day to what's most important. Now, I realize that as a volunteer you might not block each day around your commitment to youth ministry, but it's helpful to see how many hour blocks you devote to your ministry to teenagers.

Organizing your daily life into blocks, like doing a financial budget, will reveal if your time is over budget or under budget. As you write each day's activities into blocks of time, you'll see if you are doubling efforts, wasting time, or switching priorities from what's most important to what's easiest. Time management will not only make you a better volunteer but also make your entire life more manageable.

What follows the setting of priorities is rearranging the way you spend your time so you can experience your priorities. Warning: You may need to make big changes in order to focus on what matters most to you. You may need to cut a few good and worthy uses of your time for the sake of being healthier and more balanced. Take time to identify what is important, and then make room for those priorities. Do you have some shifting to do? Are there areas of ministry you may need to give up?

As a volunteer, you need to understand that time management and life balance won't happen overnight. It's a lifestyle—a difficult, ongoing process of growth that requires constant attention and evaluation. Finally, keep in mind that God adds only the things that are life-*giving*—never life-depleting.

MANAGE YOUR PRIORITIES AND TIME

CONNECT to God's Word

"For six years sow your fields, and for six years prune your vineyards and gather their crops. But in the seventh year the land is to have a sabbath of rest, a sabbath to the Lord. Do not sow your fields or prune your vineyards. Do not reap what grows of itself or harvest the grapes of your untended vines. The land is to have a year of rest." —Leviticus 25:3-5

According to these verses, work is good. God created the land and humans to work the land. However, even the land has been given boundaries by God. Even the land has a stopping point. If God designed the land to need rest, how much more do you think he designed *you* for rest?

- What seems out of control in your life? What seems to be missing from your life?

- What might God want you to take out of your schedule? to increase in your schedule?

Write a response and prayer to God here…

TO THE POINT

- Learning to manage your time is a process.
- Define what is important to you.
- Don't be afraid to shift things around so your time is spent on the essentials.

TRY IT

Design a time sheet for your monthly personal commitment to youth ministry. Do you know how much time you spend on programs (Sunday school, midweek Bible study, and so on), talking with students, going to meetings, and other commitments? Once you've quantified your time allotment, set *specific* goals for things you would like to see happen during the time you can give that month. Use alone time to honestly assess what you've done and what you'd like to do. Be realistic, but also write in an amount of time for each ministry goal so you can make your ministry more effective while still maintaining your priorities.

Here's an example:

January: Spend a one-on-one relational time with each girl in my small group.

February: Big month at work—youth ministry should focus on less student times and more notes, e-mails, and phone calls. No meetings this month.

March: Write a Bible study according to the needs of my group—enlist students to help.

April: Attend mission trip with youth group.

May: Finals are approaching—no weekly meeting. Dinner at my house; we'll cook together.

June: Family vacation month—no extra ministry commitments this month!

MAKE IT PERSONAL

MAKE THE MOST OF TIME WITH STUDENTS

from Doug Fields

FOR STARTERS

How do you spend your time with students?

When you're with students, what can distract you from being fully present?

IN THE TRENCHES

Scott is a small-group leader in our ministry, and he's also a father of four boys. He is a committed family man but also very dedicated to his small group of freshman boys. Scott spends two hours a week leading his small group. He doesn't have much additional time to give, so he works really hard to make those two hours with his guys really count.

Scott spends time during his week (usually while driving home from work) thinking about making the most of his two hours. He is organized, creative, and dedicated to giving his full attention to those freshmen during their time together. Because Scott makes the most of his time, his students don't really require much more from him. They know he's very intentional with his small-group time and is always encouraging them, asking about their faith, and pointing them to God's Word.

How are you like Scott already? How can his example inspire you in your ministry?

TRAINING on the GO

Time is precious for the students you work with. Like you, they're juggling friends, school, extracurricular activities, sports, family, work, and on and on. Therefore, it's vital that you make the most of the time you have with your students. Please don't feel guilty about what you're not doing with students; instead, be concerned about what can happen when you're with them. Time spent wisely with students leads to stronger relationships, deep spiritual growth, and authentic Christian community.

I'd like to share three tips for making the most of your time with students:

Use your time to care about their spiritual journey. Help students understand that their faith is a journey—and a journey is different than a race. They won't have instant spiritual maturity and arrive at deep places of faith by the end of the semester. An understanding of this truth can give them hope. You can care about them when you use your time to encourage them in their spiritual journey.

When you regularly ask tough questions about their spiritual growth and show an interest in their faith, they'll feel a healthy pressure to prioritize their relationship with God. Every week when I'm leading my small group of students, I ask each student how he or she connected with God since last week's small group. Since students know I'm going to ask every time we're together, they are a little more intentional about pursuing God.

Use your time to point them to God's Word. Students are constantly searching for life's answers; the good news is that you can give them more than your opinion. As youth leaders, we have the incredible privilege of pointing students toward the Bible and helping them develop an appetite for God's Word. When you and I are gone from their lives, Scripture will remain; so it's essential we encourage them to read, explore, and discover God's truths.

Use your time to provide encouragement. When you spend time with students, they're dying to hear words of encouragement. While this may be more difficult with some students than with others, you need to creatively find ways to inspire them to become what they *can be* instead of criticizing them for what they *aren't*. You can affirm students in the areas of their faith, family, character qualities, school achievements, good choices, extracurricular pursuits, special accomplishments—the list goes on and on. Basically, be liberal with your praise. When you pour affirmation on students, you spur them on to continue developing the particular area you've encouraged.

MAKE THE MOST OF TIME WITH STUDENTS

CONNECT to God's Word

"O Lord, you have searched me and you know me. You know when I sit and when I rise; you perceive my thoughts from afar. You discern my going out and my lying down; you are familiar with all my ways. Before a word is on my tongue you know it completely, O Lord." —Psalm 139:1-4

Take a few minutes to read through the entire chapter of Psalm 139. Thank God for knowing you so well and for loving you, despite what you may try to hide from him. Ask him to tell you what he specifically likes about you. Confess to God what you have tried to hide from him.

Write a response and prayer to God here...

TO THE POINT

- Be strategic in planning what you'll accomplish in the time you have with students.
- Share life with students, challenge their faith, and direct them to God's Word.
- Look for the good in students' lives, and point it out. Be liberal with your praise.

TRY IT

Depending on the time you have, try one of these suggestions for making the most of every minute.

If you have an extra	you can
5 minutes a week	write an encouraging note to one student.
30 minutes a week	phone a few students for a "Just because I was thinking about you" call. Try to pursue one significant conversation.
1 hour a week	attend a game or event in which one of your student is a participant. Make notes about the student's behavior, performance, friends, involvement, and so on. Then turn what you observed into an affirmation. Example: "I love meeting your friends; I can tell by their character that you've done a good job of picking friends."
2 hours a week	hang out with a student. Take him or her to lunch or coffee, and after a few minutes of catching up, ask how you can help him or her grow spiritually (and then be sure to follow through!).
3 hours a week	find and adapt a creative Bible study for the students you work with. Think through the needs of your students, and plan for something interactive, fun, and challenging.

MAKE IT PERSONAL

BE WISE WITH YOUR TIME

from Doug Fields

FOR STARTERS

What's your strategy, if any, for managing your ministry time?

What do you consider to be time wasters or distractions?

IN THE TRENCHES

Jennifer is a talker. She is a college-age volunteer and definitely has the gift of gab. Each week she would stop me to give me updates on her ministry, her life, and her favorite TV shows. I really do value and love Jennifer's heart for students and for our ministry. But each week when I saw her walk into the room, I began preparing myself for a long conversation. Unfortunately, the conversations would happen at the same time students were arriving. I knew Jennifer's heart is in the right place, but I also knew that I was losing a lot of valuable time for students.

I finally realized it wasn't Jennifer's fault that she was wasting my time; it was mine. I was expecting something from her that I never actually explained to her. So I had a much-needed conversation with Jennifer, telling her simply that I enjoy seeing her each week but can't always take my attention away from students to listen to her. I asked if she would consider stopping by my office once a month or sending me a weekly e-mail update on what's happening. I told her I want to cheer on her ministry, but I also want (and need) to talk to teenagers.

That honest and direct conversation was valuable for both of us; Jennifer is still able to follow through on her good intentions, and I'm able to protect my time with students. Who are the Jennifers in your life? What steps can you take to protect your time with students?

TRAINING on the GO

Your time as a volunteer is precious, so I encourage you to be wise with each minute you spend doing youth ministry. Consider these actions:

Think stewardship. Let's face the reality of time. Everyone has the same amount (7 days, 24 hours, 60 minutes). We can't make more time, so we've got to manage the time God has given us. I'm not asking anyone to become a time management guru in order to work with teenagers. But I am asking volunteers to carefully consider their time. If you can give the youth group only 60 worthwhile minutes a week, thank you and God bless you! Consider your time a gift from God, and be a good steward of it.

Debrief your time. One way to become a good steward of your time is to look back at each week and evaluate how you spent it. But don't grade yourself a failure each week for wasting time. Instead, do an honest evaluation, and then debrief.

Tell yourself something like, "OK, next week I'm not going to spend 30 minutes with that needy adult who always traps me. As much as I'd like to help, I've got to use my time with students. I need to make sure someone is caring for that needy adult, but it doesn't have to be me every week."

Each week, review how you spent your time, figure out what you can learn from it, and make some notes about what you'll do the next week.

Don't be afraid to guard your time. Years ago I learned a valuable lesson: If I don't protect my time, no one will. I realized that others don't care about my time as much as I do. They don't care that I'm late to my son's game, miss dinner, or can't meet a deadline.

Because of that reality, I've learned to take more control of my time and be more direct with people. Now I might say something like, "I'd love to stand and talk more, but I'm here only 60 minutes a week. I'm in charge of the freshman boys, and I need to get in the room and begin talking with them. I'm sorry I don't have more time right now. Maybe we can set up a time to connect at another time outside of youth group."

It's amazing how understanding people are when you directly communicate your good intentions. They don't want to keep you from doing ministry; they just can't read your mind. They're going to keep talking because they think you have nothing better to do. I understand if you're a little afraid to be direct; I once was, too. Learn the lesson now. Be a focused steward of your time so that your ministry effectiveness soars.

BE WISE WITH YOUR TIME

CONNECT to God's Word

"So be careful to do what the Lord your God has commanded you; do not turn aside to the right or to the left. Walk in all the way that the Lord your God has commanded you, so that you may live and prosper and prolong your days in the land that you will possess." —Deuteronomy 5:32-33

- What distractions "to the right or to the left" tend to grab most of your time?
- How can you cut time wasters from your life? What will be the impact on your ministry with students?

Write a response and prayer to God here...

TO THE POINT

- Even good intentions can waste time.
- Review your use of youth ministry time.
- Be wise about how you spend your time.
- Be direct in letting others know that you have a goal—and limited time.

TRY IT

Put a stopwatch on your desk, in your car, or another place you spend a lot of time. You might even carry it with you. Begin timing your distractions; for a few days, push "start" and then "stop" when you're absorbed in something you'd consider a time-wasting distraction. At the end of this experiment, debrief this time, thinking through the regular and irregular distractions. What were they? Can you remove any of them? Do you need to have a conversation with any of your regular "distractions"? Then take the next step: Make room for your priorities, and work to remove the things that don't matter as much.

MAKE IT PERSONAL

USE TIME AS A TOOL

from Doug Fields

FOR STARTERS

What do you consider to be time well spent in your ministry?

List the three things that, in a typical youth ministry week, take most of your time.

IN THE TRENCHES

My immediate, angry reaction to Jason was, "You're done serving in our youth ministry." Fortunately, Jason wasn't nearby at the time. You see, Jason had decided to let one of his eighth-grade boys drive Jason's car around the church parking lot late one night after small group.

Jason was a young youth leader and in his first year of volunteering. I knew he had no previous youth ministry experience. Frankly, my initial reaction was that I'd make sure he didn't get any more experience. But after I calmed down and realized that my angry reaction could do serious damage to Jason's future and maybe our youth ministry, I held my tongue and reflected. I realized that Jason was not trying to bring down the ministry; he was simply a young leader who made a poor choice.

I knew I'd personally been in that type of situation before, and so had the leaders in the church where I became a Christian. (In fact, one leader let me drive his car when I was in seventh grade!) By stepping back and calmly responding, I was able to give Jason grace and coach him through this situation.

How does this story inspire you to handle conflict, either now or for the future?

TRAINING on the GO

Everything you do in youth ministry takes significant time; there's never quite enough time to meet all of the needs, from building relationships with students to developing your personal ministry, problem solving, resolving conflict—and so on. And what I see and hear from volunteers is that they're very busy and live in a fast-paced world. Can you identify with that?

Wisdom tells us that not everything needs to move at rapid speed, especially when it comes to ministering to students. A healthy youth leader learns how to slow down and use time wisely. Here are a few areas to pay attention to.

Take time to develop your personal ministry. Make sure you're ministering in your areas of strength and continuing to develop as a teacher and minister. As you grow in ministry, you'll develop a strong sense of your role in the life of the church, in the youth ministry, and with your students. Out of this sense of purpose grows direction and vision for how you make a difference in students' lives. Continually seek opportunities to deepen your walk with God, and use that growth to develop your personal ministry with students.

Take time to build relationships. Depending on your personality and ability to connect with students, building quality relationships with students might not happen immediately. You may need to remain faithful over a period of time to gain their trust and friendship. A helpful principle is that the more time you spend volunteering in ministry, the more teenagers will allow you into their lives. You may spend six months with them and still not have a close connection—but that's OK and even normal.

Many teenagers have been abandoned by other adults and will be slower to open up. It's sad but true. Long-lasting, healthy relationships take time to build. I know you might want to fast-forward through the in-between time to get to the deep connection, but with relationships, time is the value.

Take time to resolve problems. While I don't believe that time heals all wounds, I do firmly believe that time can give us a better perspective and help us develop people instead of destroying them. As I write this, my mind fills with images of e-mails I'm glad I didn't immediately respond to, decisions I held off on, and advice I didn't give. We've all learned from pain caused by impulsive reactions.

A common mistake people make when it comes to conflict is wanting immediate justice and satisfaction more than restoration of relationships. It's easy to act impulsively and discover later that a wrong or uninformed decision was made—and now more people are hurt.

Instead of giving in to the temptation to dispense justice and "truth" or get even, step back and beg God for a wisdom greater than your own. While you shouldn't wait too long to resolve problems, a short amount of reflection time (even a few hours) can give you the space needed to calmly consider the options. Decide how to best respond, apologize, or compromise to find a resolution—and restore a relationship.

Allow God to remind you that he is the builder of your life and your ministry. He is in control of all the little details that currently seem overwhelming and impossible to you; hear him speak words of love and encouragement over you as he shines his face upon you and your time with students.

USE TIME AS A TOOL

CONNECT to God's Word

"But I trust in you, O Lord; I say, 'You are my God.' My times are in your hands; deliver me from my enemies and from those who pursue me. Let your face shine on your servant; save me in your unfailing love." —Psalm 31:14-16

- How can you rest in God's presence? What effect will this have on your ministry to students?

- How will acknowledging what you don't—and do—have time for change your ministry? your relationship with God? other relationships?

Write a response and prayer to God here...

TO THE POINT

- Understand that everything in youth ministry takes time—instant results don't apply to students.

- Be willing to slow down within your ministry responsibilities.

- Be patient with relationships, conflict, and your personal development.

TRY IT

Set aside an hour of time. I know this can be difficult, but set it aside as an hour of *uninterrupted* time. Use this solo time to respond more fully to the thoughts in Sum It Up.

First, lay down two lines of masking tape about 15 feet apart. Slowly walk from one line to the other, putting one foot directly in front of the other foot. With each step, pause to ask God for patience to slow down and listen to him.

[Excerpted from *Transformation Stations: Giving My Time to God*, copyright © 2005 Group Publishing, Inc., P.O. Box 481, Loveland, CO 80539.]

MAKE IT PERSONAL

USE WISE DISCIPLINE

from Doug Fields

TRAINING on the GO

> ### FOR STARTERS
>
> What do you think *discipline* means?
>
> In what ways have you used discipline in your ministry?

Two visiting students arrived in the presence of a youth pastor friend of mine in the firm grip of an adult volunteer. They were accused of stealing registration money for a church event they were attending. But before the youth pastor could address the situation, someone found the money. Unfortunately, the visiting students had already learned that at this church they were guilty until proven innocent. They came to a youth ministry event at the request of a friend and left feeling unfairly accused and victimized. What a tragedy. And it was all because an overanxious (and that's putting it gracefully) volunteer responded with premature, overanxious discipline.

All youth ministries require some discipline, yet no one enjoys it. Students don't enjoy being disciplined, and leaders don't enjoy handing out discipline. (If you do, you probably shouldn't be working with teenagers.) But there are times when discipline is necessary.

Wise discipline points toward restoration and helps students understand God's forgiveness. I want to share five actions that will help you discipline students wisely.

Think before you react. Before you take disciplinary action, think through the situation. Step back emotionally, take time to understand the scenario, observe the players involved, and assess possible outcome. Overreacting and quickly reacting often lead to regrettable situations.

Make a decision before you get angry. Don't wait until you're already angry; while you're still calm, make a decision that will value the student and bring honor to God. When anger fuels discipline, there's usually pain around the corner.

Enlist help. Wise discipline often requires enlisting other leaders. Pulling another leader into a discipline situation can help you be sure your motives remain pure, keep your emotions under control, and give you shared wisdom that's greater than just your own. The presence of another leader lightens your burden and adds a fresh perspective to the situation.

Be consistent. Provide students with clear expectations, and then have the courage to stick to those expectations. Knowing what's expected on both sides creates a safe atmosphere; there are no surprises. When a student messes up and you respond with discipline, the student is not caught off guard, especially when discipline is done in a loving, gentle way.

Move students toward the goal of becoming like Christ. The ultimate goal of discipline is to help students become more like Christ. Another term for that is discipleship; discipline and discipleship go hand in hand. As a leader, keep in mind that *discipleship* is the end goal. When discipline is done correctly, confidently, and in a Christ-like way, you'll help students become devoted disciples of Jesus.

Discipline should, at its very foundation, be built on love. So base your discipline on concern for students and never on anger. Love, compassion, gentleness, and selflessness are the building materials of discipline.

IN THE TRENCHES

Jeff is a veteran volunteer who loves students almost as much as he loves Jesus. Discipline is usually not a problem during our Sunday morning program, but one weekend some overly talkative students got the best of Jeff. They were distracting the rest of the group during a key moment; Jeff stood up and insisted that the disruptive students leave the room. Unfortunately, Jeff hadn't taken time to think before he reacted in anger and found himself in a battle of wills. Jeff was correct in that the excessive talking needed to be addressed, but his quick actions escalated the problem.

One student stormed out of the room in embarrassment, while the others stayed where they were. Jeff sat back down, but he was very angry and struggling to keep a healthy perspective. Because Jeff had reached the point of anger, he should have asked another leader for help with the situation. I know Jeff well enough to know his heart was right; however, his reaction was wrong. If Jeff had been his normal, consistent self, he would have politely asked them to be quiet or guided them outside to talk. If the noise was not out of control, he could have pulled them aside after the service to talk with them about being respectful.

How have your reactions to students been like or unlike Jeff's?

USE WISE DISCIPLINE

CONNECT to God's Word

"My son, do not despise the Lord's discipline and do not resent his rebuke, because the Lord disciplines those he loves, as a father the son he delights in. Blessed is the man who finds wisdom, the man who gains understanding." —Proverbs 3:11-13

- How can you link this passage to the ways you choose to discipline students?

- In what ways can you implement wise and loving discipline? How can you keep the end goal in mind?

Write a response and prayer to God here...

TO THE POINT

- Don't let anger take over a situation.
- Be willing to gently love students through tough situations.
- Discipline with an end result in mind.
- You can't have discipleship without discipline.

TRY IT

Read Proverbs 2, and then go on a prayer walk as you think about what this Scripture says about wisdom, understanding, and discipline. Take some time to reflect on past discipline decisions you have made. Travel through questions like these:

- What resolution do you need to make with a student or another leader?
- What current discipline situations are you dealing with? How will you handle them?
- How can you grow in wisdom and understanding?

Ask God to help you lovingly discipline with the end goal in mind, which is helping students become devoted followers of Jesus. Finally, commit to some practical steps you would like to take to carry out wise discipline in ministry.

MAKE IT PERSONAL

BE A LEADER BEFORE BEING A FRIEND

from Doug Fields

FOR STARTERS

What leaders have had an impact on your life?

What qualities do you respect in those leaders?

IN THE TRENCHES

Diane and Melissa were very close. Diane had been Melissa's small-group leader for two years, and in that time they had built a strong adult (Diane)-to-teenager (Melissa) friendship. Because they were so close, Melissa often confided in Diane about the things happening in her life.

One day, Melissa told Diane that she was struggling with an eating disorder. Melissa asked Diane not to tell anyone. Diane really struggled with this request. She wanted to respect Melissa's privacy, but she knew that Melissa's eating disorder was very serious and harmful. So Diane told Melissa that she couldn't keep the eating disorder a secret and that she would help Melissa tell her parents and walk by her side through any needed treatment.

Melissa was angry and hurt because she felt she'd been betrayed. Diane lovingly explained that she understood but had Melissa's best interest in mind. Because of her responsibility as an adult leader, she had to put aside being a friend to make sure Melissa's parents were involved and the proper steps were taken. Melissa did tell her parents, and Diane stuck by her, loving her through the recovery process. Diane did the right thing as an adult leader, and eventually her friendship with Melissa was restored and became stronger than ever.

TRAINING on the GO

One of your goals as a youth leader is to have strong and healthy relationships with students. However, it's important to maintain the difference between being a leader and being a friend. Problems can appear when those roles are reversed.

Most students have enough buddies in their lives and aren't actively looking for adults to be their best friends. A friendship with a caring adult is a by-product of a relationship-based youth ministry, and it's very important. But students need adults who are willing to lead them through life's tough situations. Anyone can be a buddy. It's difficult to be an adult leader in a teenager's life.

Since the leader-friend boundary is often difficult to discern, let's consider some differences.

A friend-first youth leader will obsess over whether students think he or she is cool. This youth leader might get overly passionate about teenage issues and side with students when they have disagreements with their parents. A friend-first youth worker might hesitate to challenge students to grow deeper in the faith.

A leader-first youth leader doesn't care as much about being liked but is trusted and respected, asks tough questions, and looks out for the students' best interests. While friends may emulate *some* of these qualities, leaders have all of these qualities. Don't get me wrong: A leader may resemble a friend, but the big difference is that the leader knows where to draw the line.

Students need adult leaders who will give practical direction, biblical guidance, and ongoing care. While students' reactions may be hurtful at times, they do respect an adult who provides difficult guidance in a loving way. Whether students are going through positive or difficult situations, they're looking for adults who will give helpful direction—telling them what they need, not what they want to hear.

Teenagers also need adults to give them guidance that's rooted in God's Word. Communicating God's direction is often difficult because it's not always easy or student-friendly. But students rely on adults to bring God's perspective into view. Friend-first youth workers do not often get beyond the surface of a situation before quickly turning to something else—something that's not as threatening as God's truth. Leaders need to be willing to challenge students to seek God in their daily lives. If you're not doing it, who will?

Teenagers find plenty of fake and surface relationships; they're looking for loving, authentic relationships. I want to challenge you to be something different than what students are used to. Seek to love students in an authentic, healthy way. Affirm them in a deeper way than their peers do.

Being an adult leader who truly loves students doesn't mean you won't be likeable and fun to be around. But consider *being liked* a bonus rather than your primary goal.

BE A LEADER BEFORE BEING A FRIEND

CONNECT to God's Word

"Now that you have purified yourselves by obeying the truth so that you have sincere love for your brothers, love one another deeply, from the heart. For you have been born again, not of perishable seed, but of imperishable, through the living and enduring word of God." —1 Peter 1:22-23

- According to this verse, how can you develop sincere love for your students?

- In what ways will you be a leader first and a friend second?

Write a response and prayer to God here...

TO THE POINT

- Understand your primary goal as a youth leader.
- Don't be afraid to make tough decisions.
- Work toward the balance between leadership and friendship.

TRY IT

Choose three leaders in your life whom you really look up to. Get together with each one individually to learn from his or her leadership. Begin the get-togethers by thanking the leaders for the role they've played in your life. Then, ask questions about the way they lead. For example, ask:

- What is your biggest challenge in leadership?
- What are some situations where you had to choose leadership over friendship?
- How do you lead and maintain healthy relationships?
- What do you think is the biggest reward in leadership?

As a follow-up to your meetings, choose two things that you would like to work on in your own leadership to students. Put them into action with your students this week.

MAKE IT PERSONAL

EXAMINE YOUR MINISTRY

from Doug Fields

FOR STARTERS

Can you think of a time you reached a goal you set for yourself? What was the goal? How did you feel once you achieved it?

IN THE TRENCHES

I'm currently evaluating my personal health—eating, exercise—the whole thing. The evaluation isn't pretty. I typically crash-diet to meet a weight goal; then, when I meet the goal, I rejoice for a short time before regaining the weight. I have no steady exercise routine, and a near-death experience while running a race forced me to evaluate this part of my life. (OK, maybe it wasn't near death. It just felt like it.)

My exercise is basically limited to the annual 10-kilometer Turkey Trot Thanksgiving morning. Believe me, I run this race not because of desire, but because of my sense of obligation to a friend on our volunteer team. Since I don't train for the race, I'm usually laid up for a week afterward. Then it's December and I'm around more fattening food than at any other time of the year. Plus, I've convinced myself that I'm too busy in December to exercise, so I gain a ton of weight (well, not an actual ton but very close).

Next, I begin January with strong, focused evaluation that leads to lofty goals for a healthier life, which I keep for about two weeks. Can you relate to any of this? How might it relate to your ministry to students?

TRAINING on the GO

To be effective and healthy in my youth ministry, I must constantly examine it. The problem is, examination is difficult because it often requires a change and a commitment to a new plan. Since you can probably see where I'm going with this training, I don't imagine that you're bubbling over with excitement to continue reading. I understand the potential for pain, but bear with me as I maneuver through the power of evaluating your ministry.

Every time I stop to consider my ministry, I return to the same three actions: personal evaluation, goal setting, and accountability for motivation. When you're ready to do a little youth ministry evaluation, you may find these actions helpful.

Personal evaluation. Take a little time to examine your role in ministry. Where do you feel like you're making an impact? Where do you see room for improvement? What skills do you need to develop to improve in your ministry? Are you tired? excited? bitter? unfulfilled? thrilled? What's happening in your heart? Take time to evaluate your current role and feelings related to that role.

Goal setting. How do you currently measure success in your youth ministry? What tangible result or goal are you moving toward? How do you spend your time? Unless you define some specific ministry-related goals, you won't have a standard for measuring progress. So try setting some realistic goals. They don't have to be outrageous goals (like "have a significant conversation with every teenager in our city") to lead to a more effective ministry. If the goals are not worthwhile, you won't remember them, but if the goals are too big, you may not achieve them. I ask my volunteers to write short, simple goals. For example:

- Have a significant conversation with Nathan every week.
- Pray five minutes daily for our youth ministry.
- Show up to youth group on time.
- E-mail one student from my small group each week.

My experience is that a little success with *small* goals makes me want to continue to set more and larger goals. Meeting several small goals is better than setting hugely ambitious goals that are never met.

Accountability. A goal without some type of accountability is often nothing more than a good intention. Accountability can be a great motivator. If I know another youth leader is going to ask me about one of my goals, I'm much more likely to pursue that goal. I ask our volunteers to share their goals with another volunteer for a little built-in accountability. I'm not suggesting militant accountability and confrontation. I am encouraging the type of accountability that's a simple acknowledgment, such as, "How did your conversation with Nathan go this week?"

The unexamined ministry can become a wasted ministry. And while examination isn't easy, it can have great power with a little attention and help from those you share ministry with.

EXAMINE YOUR MINISTRY

CONNECT to God's Word

"Test me, O Lord, and try me, examine my heart and my mind; for your love is ever before me, and I walk continually in your truth." —Psalm 26:2-3

- What's one step you'll take to prayerfully evaluate your heart? your ministry?
- Who will you ask to hold you accountable to follow God's leading in ministry?

Write a response and prayer to God here...

TO THE POINT

- Make the decision to evaluate your ministry.
- Don't be afraid to look close—and then set some small goals.
- Find someone to partner with for accountability.

TRY IT

Grab any newspaper, and take a moment to examine every inch of the front page. What are the different sections? What are the most important articles? What faces do you see? Who are the reporters? Spend about 10 minutes looking carefully at everything. Now take a blank sheet of paper and sketch similar sections to represent your ministry (and your life, if you choose).

Think of all the areas of ministry you're responsible for, and make boxes, headlines, or small notes for each one. Priorities should be in big boxes (think headlines), smaller priorities should be in the side column (think sports scores and weather reports), and frustrations should be in bold (think natural disasters).

Include everything that makes up your ministry to students. Now flip the paper over and draw the same boxes and sections. This time, write what you want each area to look like in one year. Set some realistic goals for these different areas of your ministry, and make a plan for achieving each goal.

MAKE IT PERSONAL

LEARN PREDICTABLE BEHAVIOR

from Doug Fields

FOR STARTERS

Have you ever taken the time to research the age group you're working with? Try it, and see what you find. Go to your favorite search engine and type in "adolescent development." Then poke around for teenage-related information.

IN THE TRENCHES

Observation can be a huge part of understanding the behavior of your students. Cody, a student in my small group, acted up every week. He would take the group discussion on tangents, make up stories, distract other students—basically doing anything to gather attention (and get our group off track). After watching this week after week, I realized Cody was just looking for approval and acceptance from the other students. His behavior reflected a deep need for attention. Once I understood where he was coming from, I tried to meet him there.

I adjusted my approach. I made a special effort to connect with Cody before small group began, and in our discussion times, I'd call on him first so he could share. When possible, I affirmed him in front of the group. This way, he still got some of the "spotlight" but wasn't the center of the group's focus.

When I realized it was better to understand him as a person than try to make him the perfectly behaved youth, life became a lot better for both of us.

Who are the Codys in your group of students? How can this story inspire you to respond to them?

TRAINING on the GO

Have you ever wondered why some students won't sit still and listen to what you have to say or why some girls can be so vicious to one another, while most seventh-grade boys have the conversation skills of cavemen? Have you ever asked yourself, "Why can't I get through to them?" or "Am I really making a difference with my time in youth ministry?" If you've ever asked any of these questions, welcome to the world of *normal* youth ministry. But don't worry. Your youth group doesn't contain a bunch of aliens, and you're not out of touch.

Think of it this way: You're dealing with bodies and brains that are undergoing huge changes. When you're confronted with behaviors you don't understand, remember that you have no control over the way a student acts. The good news is that you do have control over your *response*. Whether behavior is positive or negative, you have the opportunity to minister to students by reacting with wisdom and Christ-like character. Though you may not agree with their actions, students need to know that you still love them.

Use these tips on dealing with students who don't always act the way you want them to.

1. **Don't react right away.** Give yourself some time to think through what you want to say or do.

2. **Respond in a loving way.** I know this can be difficult, but students exist in an often-negative world, and they're used to being treated with anger, bitterness, and sarcasm. Give them the opposite.

3. **Question behavior.** Try to get to the *why*. Chances are good that beneath the surface something significant is causing the behavior.

Begin a journey to understand the age group you work with. Do research, talk to parents, question teachers, and interview students. You may never fully understand every behavior, but the more you immerse yourself in understanding teenagers, the more effective you'll become in ministry.

For example, if you know ninth-grade boys can be obnoxious at times, you won't expect them to sit calmly and listen to a two-hour lecture on the benefits of memorizing Leviticus. Your heart may be in the right place, but your understanding of adolescence may need some realism. A better goal would be to focus less on getting them to meet your expectations and more on teaching them to be like Jesus.

Let's face reality: Some students are difficult to love, hard to understand, rude, disrespectful, and wild (to name a few). If you have any of these students, you're called to love them—no matter what. Be patient with them, don't approach them with unrealistic expectations, see the good in them (and tell them about it), persevere with them through the difficult times, and encourage them.

I'm not advocating that you give up on discipline, self-control, and good behavior. I'm just asking that you lead not with a mouthful of rules but with a heart full of understanding.

LEARN PREDICTABLE BEHAVIOR

CONNECT to God's Word

"And if you lend to those from whom you expect repayment, what credit is that to you? Even 'sinners' lend to 'sinners,' expecting to be repaid in full. But love your enemies, do good to them, and lend to them without expecting to get anything back. Then your reward will be great, and you will be sons of the Most High, because he is kind to the ungrateful and wicked. Be merciful, just as your Father is merciful." —Luke 6:34-36

- Which students do you want to understand better? How will you respond to their behavior in a Christ-like way?

- In what ways can you better love your students?

Write a response and prayer to God here...

TO THE POINT

- Do your homework. Seek to understand what your students are like.

- Be quick to observe and slow to act.

- Adjust your leadership style to meet your students' needs.

TRY IT

Take an afternoon to visit your students' world. Go to a place where students hang out—a coffee shop or the mall, for example. Wherever you go, casually observe the teenagers who are there. Watch them and take notes. Pay attention to how they interact with one another, the way they talk, how they respond, what expressions they make, and especially the way they interact with adults.

Ask questions. What is that teenager's background? What might his or her relationships look like? Why does the teenager interact with people that way? How is a particular teenager like or unlike the students in your ministry?

Use this experience to better understand why your students do what they do and why they are the way they are. Then decide how you'll put those observations into practice in your ministry.

MAKE IT PERSONAL

SHARE LIFE

from Doug Fields

FOR STARTERS

Do you remember the game Show and Tell from when you were a child? If so, what do you remember about it? What were things you once got excited about showing to others?

IN THE TRENCHES

Mike is a volunteer who has an unusual hobby: He loves to fly airplanes. He's a dentist by vocation, which allows him the income and the freedom to have this type of hobby. And as a veteran pilot, he loves to fly and to teach others to fly. Plus, he's required to spend a certain amount of time in the air each year.

Can you see where this story is going? Mike's passionate about flying airplanes and spending time with teenagers—and he's very good at combining these passions. He invites teenagers and their parents to fly with him on a weekly basis.

Almost every year at our banquet for graduating seniors, students share that one of their favorite parts of being in the youth ministry was learning to fly with Mike. While no student might compare cleaning my garage with being 10,000 feet in the air, both are great examples of connecting with students outside of youth group. Mike has a plane; I have a garage. What do you have to share with teenagers? Whatever it is, figure out how to use it to enhance your ministry.

TRAINING on the GO

When I start talking to my youth ministry volunteers about sharing life with students, I quickly see questions in their tired eyes. "Doug, how much more of my life do I need to share? I already give up time each week to be with students. What else is expected?"

That's a fair response, since most youth ministry volunteers are trying to squeeze ministry time into their already busy daily lives. Can you relate? If so, I want you to know that I'm not asking you to give more time; rather, I'm challenging you to use the time you're already spending to actually *share your life* with students. And by "your life," I mean the one you live every day.

For example, involve students in grocery shopping, working around the house, running errands, or exercising. I want you to have a full life, healthy friendships, and a good relationship with your family. And really good ministry *can* take place here, "outside the lines" of the planned, weekly youth ministry programs.

Don't try to be with students 24/7. (If you are, you may need counseling—or a jail cell.) Instead, look at your week and think about how a normal errand or moment might become a ministry opportunity. Great conversations with students happen in a mundane car ride, while you're jogging around the neighborhood, or while you're cleaning out your garage.

When you learn to share life with students in simple, ordinary, everyday ways, you allow them to see your life outside of church. Teenagers need to see live examples of men and women with actual lives and healthy families and friendships. They need to see you away from the church program. They need to see the real you.

You might be pleasantly surprised at how comfortable students feel opening up to you during "normal life" times, the times they see are mixed with struggles and successes (if you're like most people). So think of things you do every day, and consider how you could involve a teenager.

I think you'll find that you'll no longer be just a teacher giving examples; you'll be a *living* example to students.

A couple of cautionary points: Be sure to think through and establish boundaries. Opening your life requires setting the appropriate limits. When you develop boundaries and don't have an all-access policy, you'll teach students something about priorities. They'll feel even more special when they're invited into your very important times.

Make sure your church and youth ministry allow for adult-to-teenager interaction away from the church property. Some churches don't allow their volunteers to meet with students in private settings. Obviously, follow your church rules and respect the church leadership.

SHARE LIFE

CONNECT to God's Word

"We loved you so much that we were delighted to share with you not only the gospel of God but our lives as well, because you had become so dear to us."
—1 Thessalonians 2:8

- What does it mean for you to share your life with students? What effect will it have on them? on you?

- In what ways can you involve a student in your everyday life this week?

Write a response and prayer to God here...

TO THE POINT

- Involve students in your everyday life.
- Let normal activities become unique opportunities for connecting with students.

TRY IT

The next time you meet with your students, plan a "share night." Whether it's after Sunday school, your midweek program, or at your small group, take some time to open up your lives to one another. As you "share life" with your students, you'll better understand what their real lives are like, and your students will get a glimpse into what *your* life is like.

You might begin with a few starter questions. Or try this activity: Have all students bring three items that represent who they are. The items can be from the past or the present. Here are some examples.

- photos of family, friends, or other significant relationships
- iPod or cell phone
- favorite book or movie
- paper from a favorite subject in school
- old toy, blanket, or baby picture
- sports equipment, hobby items, or a favorite gift

Then give each student time to talk about each item and what it means. You'll be amazed at how much your relationships will deepen by simply sharing your lives in this way.

MAKE IT PERSONAL

GIVE RIGHT ATTENTION AND AFFECTION

from Doug Fields

FOR STARTERS

Mentally list the healthy ways people give you attention. What about affection?

What pros and cons immediately come to your mind when you think of the word *affection*?

IN THE TRENCHES

When I think of youth ministry leaders showing affection, I think of two volunteers: Marla and Tyler.

Marla has been a volunteer at my church for several years. She genuinely loves students, points them to Jesus, and helps them in practical ways—through encouragement, tough love, intervention, and affection (her signature hugs). I believe the secret to Marla's success is that she shows by the way she treats students that she sees who they can become instead of settling for who they are now.

Marla's affection comes in many forms. Sometimes affection is a physical hug; sometimes it's a smile. I've also noticed her caring enough to remember a name or follow up on something a student mentioned during a prior conversation. She's mastered the ability to let students know she genuinely cares about them, knows them, and loves them.

Tyler is another volunteer in our youth ministry who makes students feel loved and valued in just a few minutes. He uses a very simple technique: laughter. Tyler's laughter is infectious; his warmth and sincerity make you feel as if you've been friends for years. He's taught me the power of a cheerful smile and a kind word. Students walk away from Tyler feeling that he genuinely cares for them—and he does.

How are you like—or unlike—Marla and Tyler? What can you learn from them?

TRAINING on the GO

Whether or not you like to admit it, you probably find it easier to give affection to some students than others. That's totally natural; some students are just easier to be affectionate with. But *all* students are in need of encouragement, attention, and affection. When I give a bearhug to one student and a handshake or a nod to another, I inadvertently communicate that I value one student more than the other.

As a youth leader, I'm trying to learn how to give equal levels of affection to all our students. Here are some guidelines I try to follow.

Show consistent affection. A few weeks ago, after having lunch with a group of female students, I hugged Melanie, who responded half-jokingly, "So you only hug me from the side, but you hug everyone else from the front. What's up with that?" Thankfully, here's where consistency brought its reward. The other teenage girls chimed in and said, "You're crazy! Everyone knows Doug hugs from the side. He's always done it that way." With that, Melanie was comforted that I hadn't shown favoritism or treated her differently.

I don't want to be legalistic in how I show affection, but I've learned over the years that it's best (for me) to be conservative in my affection and hug everyone the same way (which I choose to be a side hug). Regardless of your affection style, try to be consistent. Leaders in youth ministry are vulnerable to suspicion, and it's not uncommon for a hug and extra attention to be misperceived. Every year I run across news stories of youth leaders who didn't guard their relationships with appropriate affection, and it led to unhealthy relationships or even crimes.

Consistency plays a huge role in this area—if you're showing the same type of healthy affection to all students, you'll personally be above reproach and still make your students feel valued.

Be generous with verbal affection. It's not uncommon for a teenager to get verbally destroyed at school, at home, or with friends. (I've even seen it happen at church.) Verbal encouragement is missing from the lives of many students.

You have the opportunity to be a source of affection that isn't easily found in a teenager's world. As an affectionate youth leader, you breathe life into students by being a source of acceptance and verbal affirmation. Your encouraging words can help communicate belonging, and it's amazing to see what the power of a well-placed word is for a teenager.

When students associate you with inclusiveness, welcome, encouragement, and genuine affection, they'll be more open to a relationship with Jesus.

GIVE RIGHT ATTENTION AND AFFECTION

CONNECT to God's Word

"Love is patient, love is kind. It does not envy, it does not boast, it is not proud. It is not rude, it is not self-seeking, it is not easily angered, it keeps no record of wrongs. Love does not delight in evil but rejoices with the truth. It always protects, always trusts, always hopes, always perseveres."

—1 Corinthians 13:4-7

- In what specific ways can you live out this passage with students?
- Where are you giving appropriate, consistent attention? affection? Where aren't you?

Write a response and prayer to God here...

TO THE POINT

- Recognize that all students need affection.
- Consistency is the key.
- Set appropriate boundaries.
- Realize that affection is more than physical.

TRY IT

Take a few minutes to write all the different ways you can think of to encourage students or show them affection. For instance, "Write a note," "Give a compliment," "Affirm character," "Leave an encouraging voice mail," or "Send an uplifting text message." The more creative and fun, the better.

You might also get together with a few other youth leaders and brainstorm several ways to show your students you care about them.

Compile all ideas into a list, and keep it in your car, on your desk, or at home; allow it to serve as a reminder to be liberal with how you show affection to your students.

MAKE IT PERSONAL

ASK GOOD QUESTIONS

from Doug Fields

FOR STARTERS

How do you normally begin a conversation with a student?

What are your typical conversations like?

IN THE TRENCHES

Tracy is a super-relational volunteer at our weekend service. She loves meeting new students and helping them feel connected in a big group setting. One Sunday Tracy met Olivia. At first glance, Olivia seemed to be like any other teenager. Tracy started asking her some starter questions: "What school do you go to?" "Are you involved in any after-school activities?" "Do you have any brothers and sisters?" Olivia and Tracy began talking, and through a series of questions, Tracy learned that Olivia was in the middle of a messy custody battle because her parents were divorcing.

Tracy and Olivia ended up talking through the entire weekend service. If Tracy had stopped at the starter questions, she might not have uncovered what Olivia was dying to share with someone who cared. It was just below the surface. It takes work and patience to ask questions, but most students are waiting for you to ask the right questions. How does Tracy and Olivia's story inspire you in your relationships with students?

TRAINING on the GO

Quality conversations are an important key to building good relationships. Healthy youth ministry happens in the context of relationships. Incredible messages and awesome games, although they play an important role, won't be remembered—not like the conversations you share with students. So it's essential you become a good question asker.

During my first decade in youth ministry, I was lousy at asking good questions. I used the same basic questions to start each conversation with a new student. "What grade are you in?" "What school do you go to?" "What sports do you play?" I would never remember the answers, and the questions were only an attempt to find some sort of familiarity. There was no real connection.

Students were often anxious to escape the dorky youth worker who was playing 20 questions so they could find their friends. I soon saw that bad questions are more than ineffective—they can cause students to put up defenses.

However, effective questions communicate interest, help students feel known and loved, and even guide them to life change.

My frustration and failures finally forced me to rethink my approach to connecting with students. I identified a few question-asking goals and developed filters through which I put every possible question.

Insider questions. An insider question gets behind what's easily apparent. For instance, if you see a student with a cast on his or her arm, the typical question would be, "How did you break your arm?" It's a fine question, but the student has already answered it a thousand times. An insider question might be, "How did your parents react when you broke your arm?" This question gets me inside the mind or heart of a teenager instead of focusing on the event itself. Normal questions may break the ice, but insider questions get students telling you about the story underneath the "safe" typical answer.

So, don't waste time asking obvious, typical questions. Go for the good stuff.

Follow-up questions. When a student shares something with you, make a bridge to a deeper question. For instance, "Wow, you won your baseball game? That's amazing." Then, take a deeper path: "How does practicing during the week impact your homework?" "How do your parents respond to that?" "What would they say if you quit?"

The follow-up questions are always easier than the first insider question. Follow up with additional questions, and show that you care about the answers. Take an interest and keep digging with more questions.

Build on what you learned. When you're with students, make sure to comment on your last conversation together. Remembering conversations is as important as remembering names. Linking to past discussions communicates that you have a genuine interest in their lives. When you remember what students tell you—even if you forget a couple of details—you strengthen their belief that you value them and that talking to you isn't a waste of time.

ASK GOOD QUESTIONS

CONNECT to God's Word

"If I speak in the tongues of men and of angels, but have not love, I am only a resounding gong or a clanging cymbal. If I have the gift of prophecy and can fathom all mysteries and all knowledge, and if I have a faith that can move mountains, but have not love, I am nothing. If I give all I possess to the poor and surrender my body to the flames, but have not love, I gain nothing." —1 Corinthians 13:1-3

- In what ways can you approach every conversation with love and depth?
- How will you begin asking students intentional insider questions? What difference will this make?

Write a response and prayer to God here...

TO THE POINT

- Be intentional with your questions.
- Asking good questions takes practice.
- Follow up on significant conversations.

TRY IT

In the next week, initiate a conversation with a student you don't know very well. Before you approach the student, think through some great questions. Try to listen to what the student is saying, and ask some insider, follow-up questions that make bridges to something deeper. After the conversation ends, write notes of what you talked about. Then, send the student a note or e-mail referencing your conversation.

A sample e-mail might say,

Hey there,

It was so great talking to you at church on Sunday. I was excited to hear that you're giving a speech at school this week. You have an amazing gift for speaking in front of people. I know you'll do awesome! You said you were feeling nervous, and I just wanted to let you know that I'll be praying for you on Wednesday. If you think about it, call me and let me know how it goes. If not, can't wait to hear about it next Sunday!

MAKE IT PERSONAL

CELEBRATE THE MILESTONES

from Doug Fields

FOR STARTERS

What have been some significant milestones in your own life?

Which people celebrated these milestones with you?

IN THE TRENCHES

Misha is a grandmother who doubles as a small-group leader in our youth ministry. And she *never* forgets the birthday of any of the girls in her group. In fact, she goes a little crazy (in a good way) for her girls' birthdays.

Before the girls go to school on the morning of their birthday, Misha personally delivers balloons to their house. Then, she bakes each girl her own birthday cake and brings it to small group for everyone to enjoy.

Misha also takes the time to make a special, handmade birthday gift for each girl (last year, she knitted scarves). Misha understands the importance of milestones. She knows birthdays are a big deal to teenage girls, and she goes the extra mile to celebrate them and make each girl feel special. How are you like or unlike Misha? How can she inspire you to celebrate milestones?

TRAINING on the GO

One thing a thoughtful youth leader does is take time to recognize teenagers' significant life events. Acknowledging milestones endears you more personally to students and their families. And since ministry happens best in the context of relationships, your personal ministry with students will have more impact when you make this effort. Think about it: Who doesn't like to be recognized and praised for accomplishments?

Now, keep in mind that not all students will react with enthusiastic and open appreciation when you recognize them. But you can be sure they'll be beaming with pride and gratitude (on the inside) when you celebrate significant moments in their lives.

Milestones come in a variety of types and styles. For some students, it'll be athletics, academics, drama, music, or another kind of extracurricular activity. For other students, it'll be a stage-of-life milestone, such as getting a driver's license or graduating from junior high or high school.

Teenagers are also reaching frequent spiritual milestones. Some of these milestones are relational in nature; some are rites of passage, renewed commitments, lifestyle changes, overcome temptations or hurtful habits, and the healing of pain. Recognizing spiritual milestones is essential in helping students better understand their own spiritual journey, especially because many teenagers may not even be aware of their milestones.

You may also have students experiencing painful milestones—for instance, a death in the family or the breaking off of an unhealthy relationship. Recognize these milestones, too, but make sure the students are OK with you bringing attention to them.

When your students experience a milestone,

- pile on the praise. When appropriate, praise the students in front of others—and be specific with your praise.
- involve other students and peers in the celebration process.
- invite parents to participate and celebrate the victory moments.
- have students share their story as an inspiration for others.

Try to be aware of, and track, your students' milestones. Celebrate the joyful milestones, and help them navigate the difficult ones.

CELEBRATE THE MILESTONES

CONNECT to God's Word

"The Lord your God is with you, he is mighty to save. He will take great delight in you, he will quiet you with his love, he will rejoice over you with singing." —Zephaniah 3:17

- According to this verse, how is God at celebrating milestones? What does this mean to you in your life and ministry?

- How might you more intentionally celebrate your students' milestones? Why is this important?

Write a response and prayer to God here…

TO THE POINT

- Celebrate personal and spiritual milestones.
- Pile on the praise.

TRY IT

Make it a habit to gather smooth rocks or garden stones. If you can't find them free (legally), you can buy them at a hardware store. Use a marker to write "MILE" in big, bold letters on one side of each stone you collect.

When one of your students reaches a significant milestone in his or her life, give him or her a "mile" stone. On the other side of the stone, write a few words that personally acknowledge this particular milestone. This can become an easy tradition for your youth ministry and will make a memorable keepsake for your students. Even if your students only say, "Wow…thanks…uh, a rock…neat…I guess," just recognize that this may be one of those memory makers that'll mean more to them later than it does now. That's OK; good youth ministry is all about being future-minded, too.

MAKE IT PERSONAL

DEALING WITH CONFLICT

from Doug Fields

FOR STARTERS

Think of a conflict you had with another person. How did you deal with it? How did the other person deal with it? How do you feel thinking about it now?

IN THE TRENCHES

Noelle is a high school senior who co-leads a small group of seventh-grade girls in our junior high ministry. This is her first year of leadership in youth ministry, and it has been a year filled with enormous conflict.

Noelle's group of girls split into two groups of best friends, and the two groups don't get along. Also, her group members have *highly involved* parents who passionately believe they know what's best for everyone in the small group.

As a young leader, Noelle has struggled each week to resolve the numerous conflicts. But something I love about Noelle is that she's not afraid to ask for help. She knows she's new to youth ministry and *really* new at working with parents. In the beginning of the school year, Noelle would seek counsel and wisdom every time she faced conflict; she called or e-mailed with questions and had the maturity not to act too quickly in any situation. Thankfully, as the year progressed, our ministry team heard from Noelle less and less (and not because she had quit).

We've seen her grow in this area of ministry and become a great small-group leader. Because Noelle took steps to approach conflict wisely (and not alone), she has gained confidence to deal with future conflicts. How are you like or unlike Noelle? What can you learn from her story?

TRAINING on the GO

Unfortunately, life (and youth ministry) isn't free of conflict—as nice as that would be. But it's not all bad; in every conflict you have with a student, there comes an opportunity for a teachable moment.

Your conflict-resolution decisions will affect your ministry effectiveness and have a lifelong impact on others. If you haven't already experienced conflict in ministry, it's right around the corner and coming your way soon. Are you prepared to handle conflict in a way that will bring honor to God and health to your youth ministry?

Before responding to a conflict, first decide whether the problem is worth your time and attention. In many conflicts, although I was unhappy about the situation, I decided the conflict was not worth an argument. I've learned (and continue to learn) to let some things go. If we seek wisdom and give attention to only those conflicts that must be dealt with, we'll be taken more seriously in the long run.

It's always a personal call based on values and convictions; some things bother me that wouldn't bother you and vice versa. But both of us need to develop criteria for filtering potential conflicts, and we need to discover the balance between confronting and avoiding further conflict.

Here are two suggestions. First, ask yourself, "What's the worst that can happen if I don't step in and make this a conflict?" Second, ask the opinion of a neutral third party, since the closer you are to the situation, the stronger your feelings toward it tend to be.

If you do decide an issue is worth your attention, consider carefully how you should respond. Your right response is essential. To illustrate: If you use a hammer to kill a mosquito on your friend's arm, your friend is going to be angrier about your method than about having to deal with a mosquito. So try to handle conflict in a way that helps both sides welcome an agreed upon resolution.

I ask my youth ministry leaders to try their best to resolve conflict in person. The best approach is often to withdraw from the situation, gain time to think, and then calmly engage in dialogue with the other person. The problem with other methods of conflict resolution—e-mail, phone calls, voice mails—is that you can't really un-send an e-mail or take back a message on an answering machine. And helpful nonverbal communication can't come into play. When you handle a conflict in person, words are typically chosen more carefully and body language can help communicate what you don't verbalize.

So, make it a goal to become more strategic in how you deal with conflict. Your students will benefit and your youth ministry will be a healthier place.

DEALING WITH CONFLICT

CONNECT to God's Word

"Let us therefore make every effort to do what leads to peace and to mutual edification."
—Romans 14:19

- How can you live out this verse in your ministry to students?

- In what ways will you improve how you deal with conflict?

Write a response and prayer to God here...

TO THE POINT

- Every conflict has potential for powerful ministry impact.

- Assess the seriousness of the conflict before diving in with a battle-type solution.

- Whenever possible, resolve conflict in person.

TRY IT

Find two magnets and hold them close, same-type sides together. They repel each other, right? Now, turn one magnet around; they should stick together. (This probably isn't the first time you've noticed this characteristic of magnets, so I hope you won't get lost in the wonder of science.)

Next, put the magnets on a bookshelf, in your car, or on a counter where you'll see them frequently over the next month. Use the magnets as a symbol of conflict, and for the next month, think about your conflict-resolution style. Whenever you see the magnets, consider these questions:

- Do you want to be the type of person who repels or the type who brings people together?

- Think about the different relationships in your life: Are there any areas of conflict that you need to resolve?

- What's a first step you can take to seek a healthy resolution?

MAKE IT PERSONAL

GUIDE GOOD PERCEPTION

from Doug Fields

FOR STARTERS

What positive and negative perceptions are you aware of about the following people:

- church leadership
- "venerated" church members (senior citizens)
- parents of students
- the community (in general)
- teenagers who don't attend your church

IN THE TRENCHES

Carrie was a small-group leader who loved to use media clips to illustrate what she was teaching each week. One week, she showed a clip from a popular television show.

One of Carrie's students came home from Bible study that night and told her mom that they had seen an episode of this particular show. The mom jumped to conclusions, thinking angrily that the show had replaced Bible study. She soon left me quite a heated voice mail. When I called Carrie to investigate, she was really surprised at the mom's response and told me that her group had had one of the best Bible studies of the year. She said she showed a two-minute clip that perfectly communicated the night's point and sparked great discussion. She also said she screened the clip ahead of time and made the decision that it was appropriate for her girls.

So, Carrie's Bible study had a great night—but a *clip controversy* led to a perception that she was an immature leader. I supported her decision to show the clip but used that opportunity to coach Carrie on how she might have more clearly communicated to her students' parents. How can you identify with Carrie's situation?

TRAINING on the GO

Since most people don't take the time to check out all the facts, a perception is usually taken as truth. And this applies to the youth ministry you volunteer with. For instance, if one leader says something as simple as, "Bible study wasn't good tonight," a perception is created. Some people might now believe the youth ministry has lousy Bible studies or that one of the reasons the youth ministry isn't growing is the Bible studies are bad.

You might be thinking, "Wow, that's quite a stretch from what was said." It is a stretch, but that's how some people in the church communicate. They'll hear or see one thread of truth and use it to make a case that supports their feelings. Perception becomes fact in the minds of the uninformed.

Here's a real-life example. Chester is a solid volunteer who accidentally tested the waters of perception in our church one day. One of our students thought it would be fun to sneak a ride behind Chester's car by holding on to the car's bumper while riding his skateboard. Because the boy crouched down, Chester had no clue this was happening. The boy was completely out of sight. As Chester left our church parking lot, some of our church elders saw him (a lawsuit waiting to happen). Chester even waved at them as he drove past them. (Can you see it? He's waving at the church elders while towing a student from his bumper!)

The *reality* was totally different from the *perception*, which was that Chester was irresponsible. And since Chester is part of my youth ministry team, the elders concluded that I must be a bad youth pastor.

The goal for youth leaders is to do ministry in such a way that everyone outside your ministry has no choice but to think highly of the youth ministry.

Realize that everything you do in ministry is being watched. Before this chases you away from youth ministry, consider that it's not your burden to deal with alone. Your lead youth worker and the others on the team play a role in creating and contributing to perception, too. However, it's your responsibility to think through the perception of *your personal* ministry to students.

Consider this: The way you spend time with students, and participate in events are all factors in perception. I constantly remind leaders to beg God for wisdom because it only takes one negative incident to tarnish a ministry's image.

Some examples of negative incidents I've seen include allowing students to have a food fight at church or at an event or participating in it, leaving a mess in the youth room for someone else to clean up, driving as if the church parking lot were the Indy 500, borrowing the church van and bringing it back filled with trash and with no gas, and sitting together in a church worship service and talking during the sermon.

I'm sure you could add to this list. It's important to continually think about how your ministry is negatively or positively impacting others. When you help improve the image of your ministry, you also increase the support others are willing to give your youth ministry. And that's a big deal.

GUIDE GOOD PERCEPTION

CONNECT to God's Word

"The way of a fool seems right to him, but a wise man listens to advice." —Proverbs 12:15

- What have you said or done that may have contributed to a negative perception of the youth ministry? a positive perception?

- How can you tangibly guide positive perception this week? Whom will you talk to about it?

Write a response and prayer to God here...

TO THE POINT

- Actions always create perceptions, whether positive or negative.

- Positive perceptions aren't sustained without intentional efforts.

- Work with the lead youth worker and other volunteers to guard the perception of your youth ministry.

TRY IT

Ask your lead youth worker if you can head up a churchwide "cleanup day." Invite students to spend a morning doing service projects around the church. Here are some examples of possible needs you can meet together:

- clean bathrooms
- paint classrooms
- pick up trash
- move furniture
- help with landscaping

The possibilities are endless—not only will this help your church and create a serving opportunity for your teenagers, but it will also enhance the perception of your students and your youth ministry. It's an awesome sight for church members and leaders to see students in action, caring for your church in tangible ways. And it's great for your teenagers to understand that it's "their" church, too, and they need to learn how to be good stewards of what God has given them.

MAKE IT PERSONAL

LIVE UP TO RESPONSIBILITY

from Doug Fields

FOR STARTERS

What are three things you're responsible for in your daily life?

What would happen if you were to "flake" on one of those responsibilities?

IN THE TRENCHES

At the end of our third day in Mexico, I got a call to go rescue one of our vans, which was stuck in the mud. When I arrived at the scene, I saw a damaged van; a very scared youth leader; and some students who were holding their heads, bleeding, and lying around obviously hurt.

Getting to the bottom of the story, I discovered that Tanisha—the youth leader—had been speeding down a dirt road and swerving back and forth because the students in the van were telling her to "drive faster." She gave in to the pressure, thinking it would raise her "fun meter" in the teenagers' eyes. Well, she ended up losing control and driving the van into a vineyard, destroying three rows of a 100-year-old vine.

No one was seriously hurt in the incident, but we ended up paying for the situation—not only financially, but also in terms of the trust of parents and others in our church congregation.

What can you learn from Tanisha's situation?

TRAINING on the GO

Consider the amount of faith it takes for parents to entrust their teenagers to your care for a weekend retreat or even a couple hours of Bible study.

Here are a few thoughts to get you thinking about this vital responsibility.

Be responsible with care. It's important that you be responsible with students' emotional and spiritual well-being. You're not simply "adolescent-sitting"; you're caring for the well-being of a tender young life. I ask my volunteers to focus not on big growth numbers but on each individual life and soul that God cares for so deeply.

When my son Cody came home from a junior high camp, his cabin counselor told me, "Cody is such a good kid that I didn't even have to watch him." Yikes! I wanted to say, "You didn't watch him? What were you thinking? Actually, you weren't thinking!" I knew the comment was meant as a compliment, but it was definitely the wrong thing to tell a parent. Teenagers need to be cared for. And that care needs to be communicated.

Be responsible with confidentiality. A good leader is one whom students can trust and confide in. Building trust takes time and consistency. Knowing they can trust you helps students feel safe, and safety is essential to a teenager.

Let students know that you'll respect their privacy and value their desire to share but that, in your relationship with them, nothing can be totally confidential. If a teenager tells you about something that may potentially harm the teenager or someone else, you have a responsibility to share that information with the appropriate authorities. (In most states, it's the law.)

Be a responsible listener. A cautious listener doesn't react immediately, so take time to discern the situation before you speak. A student could be sharing something with you at the height of an emotional situation. Be slow to respond until you see a clear solution. As you listen, recognize that there are always two sides to every story. For instance, when a teenager tears into his or her parents' character, be a cautious listener, realizing the parents' side of the story is probably different from the one you're hearing.

Be responsible with basic safety. This might seem obvious to you, but I've seen many youth leaders make mistakes because they allowed students to do something silly, assuming, "Oh, they know better. They won't really run into traffic." Don't assume when a teenager's safety is at issue.

- *Take traffic laws seriously.* When students are in your car, use seat belts and don't cram eight students into four seats. You get the idea.

- *Think through all outings.* Make sure you're aware of your surroundings and all possible outcomes.

Choose responsibility over student approval. If you're building authentic relationships with your students, they'll still love and respect you even when you have to "lay down a rule" or say no to stop a potentially risky situation.

As a youth ministry volunteer, you assume a high level of trust. Being responsible will benefit students, the youth ministry, the lead youth worker, the church, and parents.

LIVE UP TO RESPONSIBILITY

CONNECT to God's Word

"If anyone thinks he is something when he is nothing, he deceives himself. Each one should test his own actions. Then he can take pride in himself, without comparing himself to somebody else, for each one should carry his own load."
—Galatians 6:3-5

- How does this passage encourage you to be responsible in your ministry?
- In what ways will you commit to doing what's wise in each situation with students?

Write a response and prayer to God here…

TO THE POINT

- Being a leader is a big responsibility.
- There are two sides to every story.
- Choose responsibility (and parents' trust) over teenage approval.

TRY IT

Think of a possession that's precious to you. It might be a wedding ring, a family heirloom, or an expensive gift you received. Now, loan that possession to a friend for a few days; give instructions on how to care for it, and release him or her to watch over it.

After a few days, collect your treasured possession—and your thoughts, too. Write down your answers to these questions:

- How did you feel handing over your possession? Why?
- How responsible was the person with what belonged to you?
- How would you have felt if it hadn't been cared for properly?

Now, consider: How might your feelings be similar to what parents go through when they trust you with their teenagers? What kind of perspective does this give? Gather those thoughts and feelings, and then consider how much more valuable a life is than an item—even your most precious item. As youth leaders, we are often responsible for the lives of others, and that's a tremendous responsibility.

MAKE IT PERSONAL

UNDERSTAND YOUR SUPPORTING ROLE

from Doug Fields

FOR STARTERS

Who are the people in your life who play a supporting role?

In what ways do they support you? Why is their support important to you?

IN THE TRENCHES

A few years ago, I decided to significantly cut the number of songs we sang at our weekend service. One of our volunteer leaders, Dan, disagreed with this decision and came to me to talk about it. After hearing my reasoning, he told me he supported my decision. A month later, an influential family in our church became very outspoken about my decision regarding the music.

Unfortunately, they never came to me to talk about it; instead, they spoke bitterly about me to others in the church. Dan knew this family very well and decided to do something about their discontent. He confronted them and showed his support for me even though he hadn't agreed with my initial decision. It would have been very easy for Dan to side with this family, criticize my decision, and find a sympathetic ear. But he exhibited the ultimate support, integrity, and maturity.

I've learned that support doesn't always mean agreeing with every decision. Dan disagreed yet supported me just the same. I value and appreciate this type of leader so much, and so does your main leader.

How are you like or unlike Dan?

TRAINING on the GO

The other day I listened to a voice mail from an angry father telling me that he and his family were leaving our church because I wouldn't personally disciple his son. In my particular church setting, it's impossible for me to personally disciple every teenager.

Actually, any ministry with more than a few students could consider this an unreasonable request. Even Jesus while on earth had his ministry limits—and he had the whole divine perfection thing working for him. We're all limited in what we can do, and that's one reason I work hard to build a team that shares the load in meeting needs and discipling teenagers.

At my next volunteer meeting, I shared this incident so that our volunteers could understand how important their support is to our youth ministry. And their support of our youth ministry is more than just ministering to teenagers on a weekly basis. Being supportive is also about supporting the ministry's vision, supporting me as the leader, and growing in their role to strengthen our youth ministry.

Here are a few ways you can be supportive in your youth ministry outside of your weekly commitment to teenagers.

Support your ministry's vision. It's imperative that you understand the vision and purpose of your ministry. Take some time to better understand your ministry's vision, and then educate others in your church about what your ministry is about. Your support in this area is vital to the health and success of your ministry.

Support the lead youth worker. As a volunteer, you may be responsible for a group of students, a certain event, or a specific "piece" of the youth ministry—which is great. But the lead youth worker has the responsibility of overseeing all of the moving pieces—the people, programs, parents, expectations, and more. Regardless of whether this person is paid or a volunteer, he or she is probably juggling many different needs and commitment levels. And this person needs a team of volunteers who believe in, encourage, and support him or her.

Support and fulfill students' needs. It takes an entire group of people to minister to the students in your ministry. You can further support your youth ministry by assessing the needs of your students and then figuring out how to best fulfill those needs. You can't meet every need yourself—neither can the main leader. You need a team to work together and support one another. A healthy team will begin to see the needs of students met.

UNDERSTAND YOUR SUPPORTING ROLE

CONNECT to God's Word

"But encourage one another daily, as long as it is called Today, so that none of you may be hardened by sin's deceitfulness." —Hebrews 3:13

- Why do you think a lack of encouragement can bring hardness of heart? How can you relate to this in your own life?
- What people or situations should you thank God for—even if they're difficult?

Write a response and prayer to God here...

TO THE POINT

- Understand what you're supporting.
- Share the load in meeting needs in your ministry.
- Be supportive through your ministry's ups and downs.

TRY IT

Find a way to support your lead youth worker or other volunteers in your ministry. Do a little investigative work to find out what will show support and encouragement—and then put at least one idea into action.

Consider these ideas:

- sending an e-greeting card (Be fun and creative.)
- giving the person a night off by taking over the responsibilities and allow for some restful time away
- developing a new way to explain your ministry's vision to students (Show it to your lead youth worker as a way to serve him or her.)
- offering to meet with parents
- helping with administrative work (Ask to help with something that would save time.)

MAKE IT PERSONAL

SHEPHERD STUDENTS

from Doug Fields

TRAINING on the GO

One of the word pictures the Bible uses to describe a leader is that of a shepherd. This is a fitting description for youth ministry because the students under your care are much like sheep who depend on others to carefully guide them through adolescence. Teenagers are vulnerable to emotions, fads, hormones, bad theology, and distorted messages from culture. Volunteer leaders who play the role of shepherd gently help students understand their world and expose them to God's truth.

You can shepherd students in several different ways. Think about what shepherds do: They guide their flock, defend it from attack, give it refuge, lead it to food, and offer protection.

Shepherds feed their sheep and restore their souls. Your students need you to help them "feed" on God's Word. As a shepherding youth leader, make it a priority to spend time studying the Bible with your students. You'll be reminding them of God's love, comfort, and plan for their lives. When your students are in a weary place, help restore their souls with nourishment from God's Word. Pray with them, and share Bible verses with them. Help students see that an appetite for and understanding of the Bible can be a great source of strength.

Shepherds correct and guide. Your students are occasionally going to make poor choices. That's a reality you can count on. You can play a life-changing role by lovingly offering support and guidance. Help students recognize a poor choice and understand its connection to consequences—and then guide them toward a better choice next time. With love, offer suggestions on how to continue on God's path after this poor choice—and after future poor choices.

Shepherds protect and offer refuge. Students encounter many harmful things in their world. As a shepherd, you can offer a safe place where students are known, loved, and cared for. Your very presence and caring concern present a healthy refuge from their stress, crises, and peer pressure.

Shepherds lead the lost sheep back home. When your students wander off the spiritual path, you can help lead them back to God. It's not uncommon for teenagers to explore faith during adolescence; they might even become interested in and experiment with other religions. As their shepherd, you have the opportunity to tenderly show them the way back. Some teenagers are great at getting themselves lost but terrible at making their way back home—and that's where you come in. Don't give up on the wandering sheep. Make sure they have an open invitation to church, to your small group, to youth group activities, and to an open conversation with you. Let them know that no matter how far they stray, you'll be there to help lead them back.

FOR STARTERS

Name someone who has cared deeply for you when you really needed it. How did this person show care for you?

IN THE TRENCHES

I think one of the most difficult aspects of youth ministry is watching a student stray from God. As youth leaders, we spend so much time trying to love students and point them toward God's ways that watching teenagers take steps away from following Jesus can be unbearable.

Alyssa was a student in Julie's small group during our annual spring mission trip. They met for the first time on the trip and forged an instant connection; their friendship grew quickly and continued when they returned home. They met weekly, spending time studying God's Word and talking—generally sharing life together.

Within a few months, Alyssa starting dating (her first boyfriend ever). Like many teenagers, she quickly turned her priorities upside down to accommodate this new guy in her life. A relationship with God didn't make the revised priorities list. At best, it was at the bottom of the list.

Alyssa stopped attending church regularly and lost interest in our youth activities and events. However, she kept meeting with Julie. Julie was a light in Alyssa's life, someone who cared deeply for her and who proved she would always be there. Julie has continued to love Alyssa and guide her. It's safe to assume that when the boyfriend fades away, Alyssa will remember the foundation of her faith.

How are you like or unlike Julie in your relationships with students?

SHEPHERD STUDENTS

CONNECT to God's Word

"Be sure you know the condition of your flocks, give careful attention to your herds." —Proverbs 27:23

- How would you describe the kind of shepherd you are to students? What are your strengths? your weaknesses?

- Who are two students who need shepherding? What will you do this week to help lead them to God?

Write a response and prayer to God here...

MAKE IT PERSONAL

TO THE POINT

- Shepherds help students experience God's Word.
- Shepherds lovingly point teenagers in the right direction.
- Shepherds don't give up on "wandering" students.

TRY IT

Spend some time thinking about students in your youth group. Which one would you consider to be a "lost sheep"—straying away from God?

Now think about steps you can take to actively shepherd that student. Start small. Maybe it's a simple invitation to an inexpensive meal at a fast-food restaurant or an overpriced mocha at a coffee shop. Then think through the possible conversation starters. How might you share the truth of God's love in a way that will matter?

Here are other tangible ways to shepherd students:

- Ask questions about things they're interested in, and listen to their responses.

- Take conversations below the surface level.

- Be consistent in what you do as a volunteer—attendance at youth group activities, phone calls to students, and everything you've taken responsibility for.

- Don't be afraid to challenge students toward spiritual "next steps."

- Don't bail on students when times get tough for them.

MOLD STUDENTS

from Doug Fields

FOR STARTERS

What do you think students will remember about you after they graduate or leave your youth ministry?

What do you *want* them to remember about you?

IN THE TRENCHES

I spend a lot of time at Taco Bell (I can afford the food, and I like free drink refills), and I regularly bump into my former youth group students there. I'll never forget the day I was deeply saddened when I ran into Cassie. When she was in our student ministry, she was a dedicated student leader with a shining future in terms of faith and leadership opportunities. However, during her college years she made some poor decisions that compromised her faith and shaped the rest of her life.

That day at Taco Bell, she stood before me as a hurting, 22-year-old single mother of twins. The pain on her face was heartbreaking. She told me she was ready to make a renewed commitment in her relationship with Christ. This decision, however, had nothing to do with me, our spontaneous meeting, or my previous influence on her life. The primary catalyst for Cassie's return to faith and the church was her former small-group leader, Terri.

Terri always showed unconditional love to troubled students, and that reality was in the back of Cassie's mind throughout her prodigal years. Terri loved students who were hurting, and Cassie knew that when she returned to church, Terri would welcome her and love her. Terri set an example years ago that remained with Cassie during her good times and bad times.

How are you like or unlike Terri?

TRAINING on the GO

Recently, one of my close youth ministry friends unexpectedly passed away. After many months, I'm still hearing stories from students who have strong personal memories of him. His life had an impact on their lives. What more can you ask from a life in youth ministry?

I want to help you consider what kind of influence you have in your students' lives and what kind of mark you're leaving on their hearts and minds. In youth ministry, we build relationships with students. That's what we do.

Take this concept of relationship building a step further. Begin to think about playing a role in molding students into the likeness of Jesus Christ. What's your part in that transformation process? Honestly, it's difficult to understand the how and why of God's use of adults to help students grow spiritually. We just know he does.

A couple of obvious ways you can participate in their spiritual growth are to hold students accountable and to *show* them how to follow Christ. Fortunately, we find great examples in Scripture of Jesus molding people through relationships. He spoke some hard truths regarding relationships and love.

For example, think about Peter and how he must have felt when Jesus told him, "Get behind me, Satan!" Peter had to be hurt (who wouldn't be?), but he also knew Jesus genuinely loved him—enough to speak sometimes difficult truths. Jesus lovingly instructed people and showed them God's ways.

As a youth leader, you impact students for life, helping to mold them into people who love and serve God. You do this when you instruct them, love them, and show them God's ways.

Instruct them. Be intentional about the messages you impart to students. Most important are the messages they receive from God's Word, so teach them how to explore and navigate the Bible—and help them better understand God's Word.

Love them. Teenagers need caring adults who will genuinely love them and accept them. This type of love changes people. It's often very different from the world's definition of love, since a sincere Christ-like love cannot OK mediocrity. In fact, it can be downright tough. Jesus used tough love! Tough love for you may mean speaking the truth with gentleness and then holding students accountable for living the life they were meant to live.

Show them God's ways. Make it a goal to live a life teenagers will want to follow. Teenagers are looking at you and to you; the example you set is one they'll watch—and they're always watching. By living a Christ-honoring life, you'll show students firsthand that you're an imperfect Christian on a spiritual journey and in pursuit of God's ways. Along the journey, share your spiritual victories and struggles with them, and let them know how you navigate life as a follower of Jesus.

As a volunteer youth leader, you have the privilege of impacting students' lives. You have the opportunity to gently instruct them, share God's Word with them, genuinely care for them, and help them follow Jesus. Thank you for loving teenagers!

MOLD STUDENTS

CONNECT to God's Word

"Join with others in following my example, brothers, and take note of those who live according to the pattern we gave you." —Philippians 3:17

- What are three words that describe the example you set for students?
- In what ways can you set an example this week that will be a bright light to students later in their lives?

Write a response and prayer to God here...

TO THE POINT

- Jesus molded people through loving relationships.
- Your impact on students is lifelong.
- Help mold teenagers by exploring God's Word, loving them, and living out how to be a follower of Jesus.

TRY IT

Find some simple modeling clay (like the kind children use). Begin by squeezing the clay in your hands for a few seconds. Then, think of a student you either are currently influencing or would like to influence. Allow the student's name, face, and personality to rest in your mind, and pray about this student's life and faith.

Now mold the clay into a shape or image that reflects who this student is. As you do, consider the role you play in this teenager's life, and imagine how you'd like him or her to grow spiritually. Use this time to think about how God might use you to mold and shape this student.

Chances are you're not going to create a clay masterpiece, but you will have a reminder of a student and how God might use you to mold his or her life. Keep your molded clay somewhere where it can serve as a visual reminder of that particular student and your role in teenagers' lives.

MAKE IT PERSONAL

HELP STUDENTS FOLLOW CHRIST

from Doug Fields

FOR STARTERS

What does the word *moral* mean to you?

What do you think it means to your students?

IN THE TRENCHES

We had a wonderful small-group leader in our ministry named Nancy. She lived a lifestyle according to God's Word and cared deeply about students doing the same.

Nancy ran a healthy small group and had no problem speaking truth to teenagers. But sometimes "speaking truth" turned into pointing out everything she disagreed with in her students' lives. Her group began to focus on "who is doing what wrong" and how she could fix it, instead of being about the students' faith journey and their spiritual ups and downs.

Nancy had a tough time helping students discover their own path with God. She had a huge heart for her girls, but she was missing the role of spiritual guide. She became so consumed with the "right" answers that she forgot to spend time helping her girls face big decisions, moral issues, and life's curveballs.

Do you see any of Nancy in yourself? Why or why not?

TRAINING on the GO

If you've worked with teenagers for even a short period of time, you know their young minds are very impressionable. I've watched adolescent beliefs twist, turn, and become grossly distorted by something as simple as a television show and some ideas that sound convincing.

For example, after watching just a little bit of TV, you could easily conclude that a sexually promiscuous lifestyle is normal among teenagers. The clear message is that sex outside of marriage isn't that big of a deal. The result of buying into this for a teenager can be years of incredible confusion, nagging guilt, and complete frustration. And please understand: My goal here is not to slam TV but to illustrate impressionable young minds in a world of moving (or shifting) morals.

As a youth leader, how do you get teenagers to understand moral standards? How do you get them to define and then embrace good morals? How do you instill values and have high expectations without chasing teenagers away? Unfortunately, I don't know any easy answers, but I can get you thinking about helping students adopt Christ-like ways that embrace the truths of Scripture.

Look to Scripture. As Christians, we find our ultimate authority in God's Word. Morality that isn't grounded in Scripture is simply a collection of ideas that sound right and make people feel good. As a leader, you need a personal understanding of God's Word so you can better guide students in connecting to Scripture. You don't have to be a Bible scholar to point them to God's Word, but a regular personal intake of Scripture should be a consistent part of your life.

One reminder: Please fight the temptation to give teenagers easy answers to every morally confusing situation—life isn't that simple and easy to understand. Instead, help them develop the habit of studying the Bible on their own so they'll know where to turn during difficult times.

Speak the truth. Students need to be around adults who are willing to point them toward the truth even when the truth is painful, uncomfortable, and unpopular. Teenagers see enough distortions of truth in the world around them. They want to see something different in the Christian adults and in their lives. Don't play it safe. Speak the truth.

Be a source of accountability. When students come to you for direction, hold them accountable to the truth you're discussing. After you spend time maneuvering through the issue with them, be sure to follow up with specific questions about how they're processing your discussion.

Help students learn God's "moral" standards; then lovingly help them live in a way that honors him. They need people like you to care enough to risk *not being liked* for *being truthful*. As you make this commitment, you'll find that you gain something much better than likability—respect and the joy of watching teenagers follow Christ.

HELP STUDENTS FOLLOW CHRIST

CONNECT to God's Word

"All Scripture is God-breathed and is useful for teaching, rebuking, correcting and training in righteousness." —2 Timothy 3:16

- How familiar are you with Scripture on a personal level? How will you connect to it so that you'll intimately understand God's ways?

- Which moral standards do you see your students living by? Which of God's standards will you help guide them to? How will you do this?

Write a response and prayer to God here...

TO THE POINT

- Know Scripture personally.
- Point students to Scripture to find God's ways.
- Speak the truth in love.
- Hold students accountable to truth.

TRY IT

Take some time to understand what your students are exposed to in their daily lives.

Ask some teenagers what type of magazines they read, and then buy a few. Read the articles, evaluate the images, take the quizzes, and pay careful attention to whatever advice is given (particularly on the topic of relationships).

Next, watch a few of your teenagers' favorite television shows or movies, and look for the values that are communicated both directly and indirectly.

As you read and observe, begin to think through ways you can combat the distorted messages students download every day. It's necessary to understand the teenage world before you can help guide students toward God's values, messages, and ways.

MAKE IT PERSONAL

KNOW IT'S OK TO SAY, "I DON'T KNOW"

from Doug Fields

FOR STARTERS

Quick: Without using a calculator, what does 460,789 x 287 equal? No idea, right?

How does saying "I don't know" make you feel?

IN THE TRENCHES

I wish I said, "I don't know," the first time I ever held a parent meeting. I was a new youth pastor who didn't know anything about parenting. I didn't have any children, wasn't married yet, and had no idea how to train parents to spiritually guide their teenagers. In all honesty, I should have kept my mouth shut.

During the meeting, I suffered the humiliation of seeing seasoned parents look at me as if to say, "Yeah, let's watch you try that dumb idea when you have teenagers of your own to see how it works with them." Now that I have teenagers, I realize how much I didn't know back then. In this area and many others, I make it a point to admit, "I don't know."

TRAINING on the GO

Unfortunately, many of us in youth ministry are hesitant to get into conversations that we fear will be over our heads. Pride often makes it difficult to say, "I don't know," because we want teenagers to rely on us and believe that we have the incredibly wise answers to all their questions. (Admit it.)

Let's address reality here: Students expect adults to have answers to life's problems, spiritual questions, and future concerns, but they don't expect us to know everything. No youth leader (or any person, for that matter) has all of the answers. So, saying "I don't know" is expected in some situations. I want to encourage you to get comfortable using this phrase. *I don't know* has the ability to forge a link between your honesty and inadequacy and a student's spiritual journey.

Start with "I don't know." When students ask you questions, don't be afraid to say, "I don't know. That's a great question! And I'm sure together we can find an answer." This response humbly communicates that you care about the questions and the student enough to help find the answer. That's a good message to send, and it's also a response that involves one subtle but powerful word that empowers the teenager to be involved in finding an answer. (Hint: It comes after "sure" and before "we" above—got it?)

"Knowing it all" can be costly. Avoid giving pithy, quick responses. If a student asks how many chairs need to be set out for Wednesday's Bible study, your answer won't lead to serious consequences. It's an easy question. However, an answer to a question about heaven and hell, for instance, could have eternal consequences. Easy, quick answers can be costly if they don't force a teenager to think, consider, reflect, and even research. You want your students' faith to be deeply grounded, not based on simple answers.

The big idea here is for you to learn that it's OK not to know all the answers. And it's helpful to sometimes allow teenagers to struggle a little and see what other questions appear. This results in beliefs they personally own, rather than "right" answers that pacify until pain arrives. When students are searching for answers, continually pour yourself into loving your students and pointing them toward God.

KNOW IT'S OK TO SAY, "I DON'T KNOW"

CONNECT to God's Word

"How much better to get wisdom than gold, to choose understanding rather than silver!"

—Proverbs 16:16

- If you help teach students that wisdom is more valuable than money, how will it impact their lives?

- What's one way you'll help a student discover an answer to a tough question this week?

Write a response and prayer to God here...

TO THE POINT

- Be quick to say, "I don't know, but I'll help you find out."
- Journey with your students as they search for answers.
- Don't give quick, easy answers to tough questions.

TRY IT

Ask your students what they want to learn about God or faith. Then have them take a couple of minutes to write out what they believe the Bible says about their question or topic.

Next, encourage them to find out what the Bible says about their topic. You can point them to specific passages or set them free to find verses on their own. After about 10 minutes, have students write what they discovered and compare their findings to what they wrote beforehand. Discuss the process and the results.

This activity will help your students understand that we all have more to learn and that sometimes when we don't know the complete answer, we can go looking for the answers—especially in God's Word.

MAKE IT PERSONAL

LISTEN WELL

from Doug Fields

FOR STARTERS

Remain totally silent for three minutes.

What did you hear during the silence?

IN THE TRENCHES

Have you ever listened between the lines? Not read between the lines, but actually listened? Amanda had a gift for doing this. I remember standing outside our youth room with Amanda to greet students. When we greeted one student with a "Hi, Sarah, how are you?" she gave us a typical "I'm fine" response and went inside the room.

Amanda turned to me and asked, "Is anything going on with Sarah?"

I said, "Not that I know of. She just said she was fine and smiled at us. It seems like everything is fine."

Amanda replied, "I know what she said, but did you hear how she said it? There was definitely some sadness in her voice. I am going to go follow up on that 'fine.'"

In fact, Amanda was right—there was some pain and a story in her voice. As a volunteer, Amanda really hears what students say, how they say it, and why they say it. She goes out of her way to pay attention and listen to what is beneath the surface words.

How are you like or unlike Amanda?

TRAINING on the GO

I knew a student named Heather who talked nonstop. She was very involved with our ministry, and she was always, always, always talking. Every time I'd see Heather walk in the room, part of me looked for a place to hide, while the other part of me knew I had to figure out how to really like her (I knew I could love her—it was liking her that was difficult). If she cornered me, the conversation might last an hour and it would typically revolve around…uh…well…nothing.

One day Heather asked to talk to me, which was unusual because she normally didn't *ask* to talk. She began telling me that her parents were headed for a divorce. She looked at me through tender eyes, and for the first time I realized that all Heather wanted from me was a caring adult who would listen.

She didn't want me to preach a sermon, fix the problem, or talk to her parents. She just wanted me to genuinely listen to her. It was at that moment in my ministry that I learned a powerful truth I had avoided when I avoided her. It may not seem that profound, but here it is:

All students are different. Some students talk your ear off, some never say anything, some drive you crazy, and some are polite. Some make you wonder whether their sugar intake should be regulated, and some make you wish you had an entire youth group just like them. But all have the desperate need for someone who listens well.

Here are some tips I've learned along the way to becoming a better listener:

You know you're not listening well when you…

- catch yourself thinking of a response to the very first statement out of a student's mouth—while she continues to talk.
- allow your eyes to wander from a student's face to other distractions while he's talking to you.
- don't remember a student's name 30 seconds after you asked for it.
- ask how a student is doing and then, without pausing for a response, continue talking or don't pay attention to her answer.

You know you're listening well when you…

- listen without interruption. Let your students tell you everything they want to before you respond.
- ask specific follow-up questions, not just general ones. After listening to what's going on in a student's life, ask questions that'll dig deeper.
- stay focused on the person talking. Move your conversation to a place where you're free from distractions.
- keep the focus of the conversation on the student. When you're tuned in, he or she will feel valued.

Your students aren't expecting you to have all of the answers; they're looking to you to listen. They are looking to you to really hear them and help them navigate through life. Be patient with yourself, though. Listening is an art, and it might take some practice before you master it.

LISTEN WELL

CONNECT to God's Word

"My dear brothers, take note of this: Everyone should be quick to listen, slow to speak and slow to become angry." —James 1:19

- In your opinion, how does a lot of listening and little speaking build strong relationships?

- In one word, how would you describe the way you listen to students? How about the way you'd like to listen to students?

- What's one skill you'll practice to become a better listener?

Write a response and prayer to God here...

TO THE POINT

- Be a listener. Don't rush into conversations as a "fixer."
- Every teenager needs someone to *hear* him or her.
- Give students your full attention.

TRY IT

The more you're aware of your own listening-skill level, the better you'll become at the art of listening.

Choose one of the following to help you practice being a more intentional listener:

Listen to a song. Pick a song you don't know very well. Listen closely. Try to answer these questions: How many are singing? What's the song about? What's the feeling in the voice of the singer? What themes are behind the words of the song? What would you tell someone else about this song?

Watch a TV show. Pick a show you're not familiar with. Listen to the dialogue. Try to answer these questions: What are the names of the main characters? What's the theme of the show? What's one line that really stuck out to you? Who was the least important character? What part did that character play? What would you tell someone else about this show?

Active listening is paying attention to a student talking and then recalling what he or she said. Practice your active listening skills, and test yourself on them every once in a while.

MAKE IT PERSONAL

COUNSEL STUDENTS

from Doug Fields

FOR STARTERS

Think about someone you trust. Why has that person earned your trust? What characteristics make that person trustworthy?

IN THE TRENCHES

One day Megan, a youth volunteer, began talking to a girl who asked if she could keep a secret. I'm so grateful that Megan followed the right counseling principles because the student desperately needed help—she'd been molested by her father.

As is common in such revelations, this girl was soon accused of lying by her family members and others who didn't want to believe her story. But Megan was able to stand by this student as the evidence emerged and helped prove the girl truthful.

Sadly, this girl's dad took his own life rather than face the shame of what he had done. Now this young girl has more to deal with and many years of healing and recovery ahead of her. However, because of Megan's commitment to her, she hasn't turned her back on God and is getting the help she needs. This is a painfully tragic story, and I hope you'll never have to deal with such an extreme situation. My prayer is that when a student cries out for help, you'll take the right steps to get that needed help.

How can this story inspire you in your ministry to students?

TRAINING on the GO

Thousands of years ago, Aristotle spoke of three key questions that a communicator must answer to be most effective. I've spent many years relating these questions to youth ministry.

- Ethos (ethical): Are you trustworthy?
- Pathos (empathy): Do you care about me?
- Logos (logic): Do you know what you're talking about?

Let's explore how these questions can help you counsel teenagers. Imagine that teenagers are asking you each of the following questions:

Can I trust you? Students are looking for "safe" people who will care about their personal highs and lows—people they can confide in. But before students will open their heart to you, they need to know you're trustworthy.

Here are some actions that can damage ethos.

- *Gossip.* If you have a student going through some difficult issues that you don't feel equipped for, don't be afraid to ask for help—but be careful not to gossip. You can seek wisdom from others without giving away the student's personal information. It's essential that you be wise about whom you share information with (and when).

- *Promises not to tell anyone.* While you do want to communicate to students that they can share anything with you, you can never promise in advance that you won't repeat what you hear. A premature promise to keep something private can cause you to choose between losing a student's trust and getting the student help.

Do you care about me? Teenagers are looking to confide in people who know them and will actually care about them. Your students need to know that you'll take time to love them individually, listen to them, and then respond in a genuine and compassionate way. A popular phrase that all youth leaders should memorize is "People don't care what you know (*logos*) until they know that you care (*pathos*)."

Do you know what you're talking about? Because of the nature of counseling situations, it's important that you understand the different issues facing teenagers. No formulas work for every student, but it's wise to understand some of what your students deal with. Do research on the Internet, read magazine articles, gather insight from other youth leaders, and scan books that deal with the lives of today's teenagers.

In addition, get familiar with your county's emergency child protection procedures. Together with the lead youth worker, have a plan in place if a student ever confides in you about abuse, extreme crisis situations, suicide, harm to other students, or harm to a family member. Then, when such situations arise, you'll know the right procedures and be able to properly inform students and families. Part of your education process is knowing what you don't know and what you're not capable of; it's OK and often the right move to refer a teenager to a professional when you're in a situation that's beyond your ability.

Think through these three questions in your personal ministry to students, and consider ways you can lovingly and safely counsel them.

COUNSEL STUDENTS

CONNECT to God's Word

"But blessed is the man who trusts in the Lord, whose confidence is in him." —Jeremiah 17:7

- How will you respond when a student comes to you for help—even if you don't have all the answers?
- Which teenagers should you be praying for and trusting God with?

Write a response and prayer to God here...

MAKE IT PERSONAL

TO THE POINT

- Students are looking for someone to trust.
- Avoid gossip and empty promises.
- Educate yourself about today's teenagers.

TRY IT

At your next volunteer leader meeting—or another time that you're all together—participate in the classic team-building exercise referred to as the trust walk.

The good thing about classic ideas is that most people think they're, well…classics, so they're rarely used anymore. But they can still be fresh and effective.

Blindfold all the volunteers, and have them stand in a single-file line. Have everyone link arms, and assign one person (who is not blindfolded) to be the leader. This person's job is to lead everyone on a walk wherever you are, whether it's a room, the building, or outside. Let everyone know that the only way to get through this activity safely is to trust the leader. They need to trust that the leader won't take them into any kind of danger because, as their guide, he or she has everyone's best interest in mind.

Afterward, spend time discussing the practical applications to trust in youth ministry. How can you create an environment of trust for students, and how will you communicate this to teenagers in real ways?

BE DISCREET

from Doug Fields

FOR STARTERS

How would you define *discretion*?

How much of what teenagers share do you keep confidential? How do you decide?

IN THE TRENCHES

Brian, a new leader in our youth ministry, was faced with a delicate situation in his ministry with freshman guys. He learned that one of the boys in his small group was battling depression. Brian wanted to be there for him but wasn't sure how to help, so he talked with other volunteer leaders in our ministry about what he should do. Brian's motive was to seek wisdom from other leaders, but although he meant well, the result was that others in our ministry now knew of the boy's struggle. Brian's intentions were pure in wanting to help, but he didn't seek wisdom in the right place.

Unfortunately, it wasn't long before the teenager realized that the word was out, and he felt deeply hurt and betrayed. Brian desperately tried to explain that he was simply trying to find ways to come alongside the boy in his struggle, but the damage was done.

What experiences have you had that were like or unlike Brian's? What can you learn from his story?

TRAINING on the GO

The longer you serve as a volunteer, the more likely students are to confide in you their most private thoughts and feelings. Sometimes it's difficult to know what is and isn't appropriate to keep confidential.

Discretion is essential as you both honor students' privacy and protect the youth ministry and church. Consider a few potential do's and don'ts:

- *Don't* share a student's personal story without permission.
- *Don't* talk about students' situations except in the presence of those involved.
- *Do* keep a student's confidence—unless you believe that student or someone else is in any kind of danger.
- *Do* let students know you are a safe person to share with and that you will respect their privacy.
- *Do* let students know—before they tell you anything confidential—that you'll need to involve someone else if what they share with you has the potential for someone being hurt.
- *Do* everything you can to honor the trust students give you.

Abusive situations (present, past, and future) should *always* be reported to the lead youth worker or another appropriate person in authority so that proper help can be sought. This is why youth leaders can never promise to keep things totally confidential (no matter how much a teenager may beg).

Always walk the line between respecting students' privacy and not keeping something potentially harmful in confidence. Instead of saying, "I promise I won't tell anyone what you tell me," say, "I care enough about you that I promise I'll do everything I can to help you, and that might mean not keeping all your secrets."

Use discretion when you choose to share. God doesn't want a hurt or mistake to be wasted, and he can use anyone he has redeemed to show others his grace and love. I ask my volunteer leaders to use discretion when sharing the details of their own stories with students. For example, if they were once involved with drugs, and that season of their life had some memorable and wild times, I want them to be very careful how they relate their story to students. Some stories of past behavior may appear attractive to a teenager, who might choose to use your openness as permission to try out different things (the way you did). Or a teenager might look at "recovered" adults and think, "That didn't seem to hurt them too much. I could rebound from mistakes like they did, and I've always wanted to try that." While it's good to be transparent, please also be careful not to glamorize poor choices from your past.

Teach your students to use discretion. When you're in a group situation and students are sharing things with each other, clearly communicate the need for group discretion. Help teenagers see that respecting each other, listening to each other, and maintaining privacy (with knowledge that has been shared) is an important part of living life in community.

BE DISCREET

CONNECT to God's Word

"Hatred stirs up dissension, but love covers over all wrongs. Wisdom is found on the lips of the discerning, but a rod is for the back of him who lacks judgment. Wise men store up knowledge, but the mouth of a fool invites ruin." —Proverbs 10:12-14

- What's one way you can love students through honest, vulnerable conversation this week?
- How can you handle what students share with both wisdom and discretion?

Write a response and prayer to God here...

TO THE POINT

- Use discretion when talking about your students' personal details.
- Be wise when sharing details about your own life.
- Teach your students how to be discreet with others' information.

TRY IT

Put yourself in your students' shoes. Begin by sharing something personal with a close friend. Consider sharing something that you haven't shared before or something you haven't shared very often. As you do this, try to consider the level of trust it takes for teenagers to share something personal and important with you.

Dig deep. I realize this can be a tough challenge for an adult. But when you share something personal with someone else, you grow in trust and in your confidentiality skills (since you better understand how important discretion is). Afterward, apply what you experienced and learned to your relationships with students.

MAKE IT PERSONAL

RECOGNIZE PATTERNS

from Doug Fields

FOR STARTERS

What unhealthy patterns do your students fall into? How do you normally talk to them about patterns of behavior in their lives?

IN THE TRENCHES

Stacy was a very involved student in our youth ministry. She grew up in the church and attended just about everything we did. Her dad passed away when she was very young, and she was raised by a single mom who had a very demanding job and very little free time. This left Stacy on her own quite a bit, and she chose to spend her time participating in youth group activities.

As Stacy entered her freshman year, she started dating. She was a beautiful girl and received a lot of attention from older boys. Soon, boys became the center of her free time; she would invite a different guy to come to youth group with her every few months. Each guy had a similar attitude about church and authority and religion—they were all "tough guys" and came to church only because of Stacy's prodding. Those of us who knew Stacy recognized this pattern and saw that she was headed for disaster. Thankfully, a few of our volunteer youth leaders sat down with Stacy and talked to her about how lonely she was and how hard she was working to fill her life with love and acceptance. They wanted to help Stacy identify an unhealthy pattern and reassure her that she was valued, by us and by God.

Do you know anyone like Stacy? If so, what might she need from you?

TRAINING on the GO

The longer you serve in youth ministry, the more you identify certain patterns of teenage behavior. For example, you'll likely learn to predict that the overachieving teenager with demanding parents will have a meltdown. You'll know that teenage couples who are physical in public are probably going too far in private. You'll recognize that the teenager whose home life is messy—but who insists everything is fine—probably has anger and denial issues.

If you've been in youth ministry for any amount of time, I know you're not thinking, "Wow, Doug is brilliant. How does he know that?" After seeing the same behaviors over and over, it's easy to spot ongoing patterns.

The statement "There's nothing new under the sun" is as true today as it was when the Teacher said it thousands of years ago in Ecclesiastes 1:9—especially when you really pay attention. Even though cultures have changed, the root problems are often similar; patterns repeat themselves in this decade as they did in past decades of youth ministry.

I frequently tell teenagers that nothing they can tell me will surprise me. In 25-plus years of youth ministry, I've probably heard it all and seen it all. I tell students this because I want them to know that the adult leaders do know their world and will be present when they want to share what's going on in their life. I want them to feel that they're not alone and what they're going through has happened before.

Learning to recognize students' patterns can be a great help to you in ministry. You want to be careful not to stereotype students; however, recognizing negative patterns as they emerge shows you where teenagers need help. You'll be able to discern when difficult conversations with students need to take place—and what should be said. I've found that when students suffer painful consequences of bad choices, there was often an intervention opportunity I missed. I can't tell you how many times I've thought to myself, "I saw that one coming, and I should have said something." Fortunately, that doesn't happen as much as it once did, because hindsight alerts me to current patterns and opportunities to help students.

Your students have incredible needs; trust your intuition and God's leading to spot destructive patterns in their lives. Most students want to be helped, encouraged, and freed from potentially painful decisions. My challenge to you is to pay attention to patterns, do your best to help students before they get hurt, and offer unconditional love and assistance after they've been hurt. Students need your grace to find hope and healing.

RECOGNIZE PATTERNS

CONNECT to God's Word

"What has been will be again, what has been done will be done again; there is nothing new under the sun. Is there anything of which one can say, 'Look! This is something new'? It was here already, long ago; it was here before our time." —Ecclesiastes 1:9-10

- Think of a student who's living a pattern that concerns you. What will you say or do next time you see this student?
- How will you more clearly identify patterns in teenagers' lives?

Write a response and prayer to God here...

TO THE POINT

- Pay attention to your students, and observe their patterns.
- Don't be afraid to tackle tough topics.

TRY IT

Part of counseling students is watching, listening, and observing the patterns in their lives. Think about the holographic-type images that hide a smaller pattern within a larger one. At first glance, all you see is the larger pattern, but when you look closer, the inner one emerges. (You might even search the Internet for these types of pictures and images, and look at a few.)

Consider the students in your ministry. Why do they do what they do? In what ways do they look different on the outside than they are on the inside? What's happening inside your students that's buried within a larger picture? How can you reach into their lives and help them with these hidden patterns?

MAKE IT PERSONAL

HELP STUDENTS DEAL WITH GRIEF

from Doug Fields

FOR STARTERS

What do you say to a friend who has lost someone? Try to be as specific as possible.

What are some ways your youth ministry should respond when a teenager dies?

IN THE TRENCHES

Last year, one of my students, Leigh, died in an auto accident outside his high school. Unfortunately, I'm too familiar with this type of loss, but what was unusual about the situation this time was the crowd of teenagers who went to the hospital that day. More than 100 teenagers who were genuinely close to Lee scattered around the grass and benches outside the emergency room to wait. Each of these students was experiencing a deep emotional crisis; for most, this was a first encounter with a major loss. So I called a few of our youth ministry volunteers, and we went to the hospital to be with the grieving teenagers.

All we could do was move among them, make our presence known, and let them know that we were available to listen or talk. We opened a room at our church later that night so that Leigh's friends could mourn, share stories, and share in the pain.

These teenagers were able to make the connection that we knew Leigh through the church; once that happened, they slowly began to open up. I saw them at the school, where my volunteers helped serve as crisis counselors; I met them at Leigh's home while helping to arrange the funeral; and I was with them at the burial. My volunteers and I built a tight bond with many of these students, who now attend our youth ministry because of our shared experience with grief.

TRAINING on the GO

Tragedy struck Kasey's young life when her best friend was killed in a car accident on her 16th birthday. Kasey didn't go to church on a regular basis, but she showed up at the back door one Sunday morning. Debbie, one of our volunteers, greeted her with a big smile—and Kasey instantly burst into tears. Debbie didn't know who Kasey was or why she was upset, but she wisely didn't ask questions or try to make Kasey talk. She grabbed ahold of Kasey and just held her throughout most of the service, just letting her cry and cry.

As Debbie learned Kasey's story, she understood the tears. Debbie didn't push, but she invited Kasey to meet for coffee so they could talk more. A few weeks later, Kasey showed up at church on a Sunday morning. She walked straight over to Debbie and threw her arms around her. Kasey had experienced love during her last visit, and it was strong enough to make a difference during a difficult time.

When students experience the death of someone they love, they need caring adults to be there for them, even when it's not clean and easy and when you have no idea what to do. Here are some insights I've learned over years of navigating through difficult experiences:

Silence is golden. It's OK if you don't have anything to say. Sometimes a hug in silence or an arm around the shoulder with no words is all that is needed.

Ask questions. Don't be afraid to ask leading questions that might help a student know you are someone who really wants to listen. Most teenagers want to talk during this time, but they may not know what to say. They can respond to an opening, though, and they will when a genuine question is sent their way.

Allow time for sharing. Teenagers need time to share. Let them talk. Be careful about interjecting your own opinions or stories about your own grief experiences. Stay away from easy answers. In fact, be careful about giving any answers at all.

Give them space. This is a tough balance because we don't want to back off but we do want to give grieving people space. Most youth leaders think, "I'll just back off and give them space; they'll come to me when they're ready to talk." However, hurting people usually don't want to be completely alone during a crisis. Make yourself available while still giving them some space. Be there with a hug or a phone call or just as someone to sit with.

I'm still trying to learn the implications of tragedy and figure out how to best respond. I don't have all the answers, but I do know that God will guide you in taking the right actions that express concern and love to students.

HELP STUDENTS DEAL WITH GRIEF

CONNECT to God's Word

"Then they sat on the ground with him for seven days and seven nights. No one said a word to him, because they saw how great his suffering was." —Job 2:13

- What did Job's friends understand about helping a friend in crisis? What can you take away from this into your experience with tragedy?

- How do you think Jesus would respond to students who are grieving? In what ways will you follow this example?

Write a response and prayer to God here...

MAKE IT PERSONAL

TO THE POINT

- You don't always have to know what to do.
- Just be willing to be there.
- Sometimes students don't know how much they really need you.

TRY IT

When your students experience crisis or tragedy, they need above all to know you're going to be there for them. Try this trust-fall activity with your students. You can use it before crisis ever happens in the lives of any of your students. You don't need to wait for a tragedy to establish yourself as someone who *will* be there when things fall apart.

If this classic activity has been used too much in your youth group, come up with something new. But I've discovered that some ideas that I think are "old school" are actually new to my teenagers.

Here's how it works: Have one student at a time stand a few feet in front of you, and instruct the student to fall back. Students shouldn't catch themselves or bend their knees. They must let go of control and allow you to catch them.

Each time you catch a student, remind him or her that you're there with support and love—today and no matter what tomorrow brings. Then have your students take turns catching each other. Not only is it powerful for students to know that you're there for them, but it's equally powerful for them to realize how their peers care.

RESPECT PARENTS' TIME

from Doug Fields

FOR STARTERS

How do you view your time as a valuable commodity? How don't you?

What emotions do you feel when someone values your time? when they don't?

IN THE TRENCHES

During my beginning years of youth ministry, I didn't do well at respecting parents' time. I put a higher value on getting students to youth group than on helping families maintain a balanced schedule. Honestly, I just didn't think about what it meant to have parents waiting for their teenagers. After all, I thought, the students and I were never more than 20 or 30 minutes late ending and I didn't have anywhere to go. I had saved the night for youth ministry. When we did get out late, I would meet the waiting parents and offer a contrite apology for going over our time. (I mean, what could they say? It was church, right?)

One night a mom gave me a lesson that I'll never forget. She said, "If you were really sorry, you wouldn't allow this to happen every week. If you were really sorry, you would care about my time, too." She was kind and strong at the same time—strong enough that it made an impression on me. I put myself in her situation and realized that my disrespect for her time had caused her to lose respect for me and our youth ministry.

From then on, I committed to being sure not to waste parents' time. As I kept to this new commitment, my relationship with that particular parent was restored.

How can you relate your own ministry to my story?

TRAINING on the GO

As you minister to your students each week, it's important to remember that each student has at least one parent representing him or her. Whether you lead a small group, teach Bible study, or take students on special events or trips, you are also interacting with parents.

Make sure you schedule your time with students in a way that maintains a family-friendly environment. Here are a few ideas to keep in mind when it comes to respecting parents' time.

- If for any reason you won't return on time from an event, allow students to call home as soon as you know you'll be late.

- Schedule your time with students. Whether it's Bible study or a fun night out together, take a few moments before you meet with your students to plan your time. Be sure to communicate that information with parents. Here's a lesson I've learned: Uninformed parents are not happy parents.

- Leave a little time at the end of your group or event for talking and hanging out; when it's a scheduled part of the time, you don't have to push teenagers out the door.

- Take your students to the meeting spot where parents will pick them up, and hang out there for a few minutes. This will make your good intentions clear to parents and give you an opportunity to talk with them.

- It's better for you to be waiting on parents than for parents to be waiting on you.

I realize there will be times it's difficult to end your program on time. Discussion gets rolling, students begin opening up, and then you look at your watch and think, "What happened? I can't believe we're out of time!"

Well, as odd as this may sound, I've learned that it's better to stop and help protect the families in your ministry than to spend 15 minutes more in your group time.

By respecting parents' time, you'll encourage them, build stronger relationships with them, and strengthen their family.

RESPECT PARENTS' TIME

CONNECT to God's Word

"Show proper respect to everyone: Love the brotherhood of believers, fear God, honor the king." —1 Peter 2:17

- How does respecting your students' parents honor God?

- In what ways will you better respect parents' time?

Write a response and prayer to God here...

TO THE POINT

- Parents have family schedules to keep.
- Plan your program time so you respect parents' time.
- Be family-friendly with your use of time.

TRY IT

Ministering to students includes ministering to their entire families. Take an afternoon to interview a parent of one of your teenagers; take the parent to coffee or lunch, and spend some time getting to understand the parent's family life, stresses, parenting goals, hopes and dreams, hurts, needs, and so on. You'll gain great insight to help you plan activities to do with students.

Here are some suggestions for questions:

- What does a typical day look like for your family?
- What about a typical day for your son/daughter?
- How well am I respecting your family's time and schedule?
- How do you feel when we get out late from a youth program?
- What are ways I could partner with you and encourage you?

When your meeting time ends, thank the parent for being open and generous with his or her time. Commit to taking everything you discussed into consideration and prayer. Then, before leaving, pray for his or her family.

MAKE IT PERSONAL

DON'T DRAIN THE WALLET

from Doug Fields

FOR STARTERS

Think of all the youth ministry activities you've been a part of over the last six months. Add up the total cost of these events (include meals, events, and fun outings).

IN THE TRENCHES

In my church, we tell parents we never want money to be the reason a student doesn't attend an event or trip. So, we've established a scholarship fund in our youth ministry. This fund allows us to come alongside families so their teenagers don't have to miss out on great youth ministry experiences.

Something that makes this scholarship deal a better learning experience is that we have teenagers serve at the church a few hours a week to raise a portion of the scholarship and feel what it means to give. Some people can give above and beyond with their finances, and some can give above and beyond with their time.

How does this idea inspire you to not let money get in the way of students' involvement?

TRAINING on the GO

As you build relationships with students, keep in mind that activities you do together definitely have an impact on a budget—both a teenager's and a family's. Most teenagers aren't earning all their own spending money and paying for everything themselves; the majority rely on parents to pay for almost everything. So, when you take students on outings that cost money, it's important to recognize the effect it has on their families.

I want to challenge you to become an advocate for church events that are either free or pretty inexpensive. Not everything in youth ministry needs to cost money and drain the family bank account.

Here are some simple ideas to get you thinking.

- Cook dinner in your home instead of eating out. Restaurants can be expensive and often separate teenagers into the haves and have-nots.

- Do a service project instead of doing something more expensive (for instance, a concert or an amusement park). Take your students to serve in a retirement home or at a local shelter. A service project is a free activity, and serving together often creates stronger memories than doing an entertainment activity.

- Host a movie night at someone's house instead of paying to see a movie at the theater. Rent a couple of movies, make popcorn, grab sodas and candy, and hang out in an inexpensive and comfortable environment.

- Schedule your church events between meals. For example, have students eat lunch before they arrive at an event, and then return home before dinner. This will save the family money for two meals.

- Schedule outings that are free. For example, try sports day at the local park, game night, a hike, or a swim at someone's house.

- Talk to others on your volunteer team or in your congregation who have connections. You might know people who can get discounts through a job or hobby. They can help you do what you wouldn't normally be able to afford.

- Look for places that offer a student discount, such as a school play or sporting event.

The reality is that many families struggle to pay bills. Even in affluent churches, where people give the impression of having plenty of resources, some families are deeply in debt. When youth ministry events require money, either students get left out or families make sacrifices to pay the price.

I'm not suggesting that everything in your youth ministry is free, but as you and your youth ministry become money-conscious, you'll definitely serve families.

DON'T DRAIN THE WALLET

CONNECT to God's Word

"Of what use is money in the hand of a fool, since he has no desire to get wisdom?" —Proverbs 17:16

- How can using money wisely improve your ministry?
- In what real ways can you focus on the actual time together, no matter how much it costs?

Write a response and prayer to God here...

TO THE POINT

- Look for ways to plan inexpensive youth ministry events.
- Parents are looking to save money wherever they can.
- Making memories is about the people involved, not the activity.

TRY IT

Plan a progressive dinner for you and your students. Not only is this an inexpensive event, but it'll also get families involved with your ministry. Assign each of your students a part of the meal; for example, you might break it up into beverages, appetizers, soup and salad, main course, and dessert. You can add as many courses as you want depending on how many students or families participate.

Students or families can prepare their part to serve and eat in their own home. Have your students meet at the church, and then transport them to the houses in the order you're eating the meal. (Tip: If you have more families than courses, have the families provide transportation as their contribution.)

Enjoy each course together—and personally take note of the fact that fun together is more important than an expensive restaurant (or any restaurant, for that matter!).

MAKE IT PERSONAL

GET TO KNOW YOUR STUDENTS' PARENT(S)

from Doug Fields

FOR STARTERS

In what ways has your own family shaped who you are?

How often do you go out of your way to meet your students' parents?

IN THE TRENCHES

Youth ministry drastically changed for me the day I became a parent. I had no idea how intense my feelings would be for my new daughter. She became a focus of my life, and I instantly turned into a guide, protector, and shield from all that might be harmful (or at least that's how I see it). When it was time to send my daughter to Sunday school, I couldn't wait to meet her leaders. I was excited to know the people who would be pouring into her life each week. I was thrilled that someone was going to partner with me in pointing my daughter toward a Christ-like life.

How does this story affect the way you connect with your students' parents?

TRAINING on the GO

Connecting with parents is an important step in ministering to students. You may be thinking, "I can barely find the time to spend with teenagers, and now I'm supposed to interact with their parents? How am I supposed to do this?"

I can understand these questions and the difficulty with this kind of challenge. One of my many failures in youth ministry was that I basically conducted my youth ministry in isolation from parents. Little did I know that if I were really interested in teenagers, I would also be interested in their parents—the most influential people in their lives.

Parents want to know you. Parents want to be aware of what's going on in the ministry, and they want to know the adults who are hanging out with their teenagers. But not all parents know how to go about it—and neither do most youth leaders. Take the lead by extending the first invitation to parents; let them know that you want to know *them*.

Parents shape their kids. All of your students have unique family dynamics that influence them in both good and bad ways. By making it a priority to meet their parents, siblings, and extended family members, you gain a better understanding of why your students are who they are.

Start with baby steps. I'm not suggesting that you start a small group with parents and meet with them weekly (although that's not a bad idea). You don't need to have a best-friend relationship with each parent—but you should attempt a healthy relationship with each parent, starting with name and face recognition. Most parents will appreciate your making the effort to get to know them. Just start small: You might write a card or an e-mail, telling them about yourself. When you call a teenager's house, talk to the parent before immediately asking for the teenager.

Parents want to know what's going on. Let parents know what you're doing with their teenagers. Are you doing Bible study, discussing a certain topic, or hanging out and talking about life? It's essential that a youth ministry communicate to parents both the big picture of the ministry and the small picture—what you're doing with the students God (and they) have entrusted to you. By making parents a part of your ministry, you give them an opportunity to continue the same types of discussion at home. That's one of the goals of connecting with parents—encouraging them to take an active role in their child's spiritual development.

By taking time to get to know your students' families, not only will you be better equipped to minister to your students, but you just might build some wonderful friendships with parents in the process.

GET TO KNOW YOUR STUDENTS' PARENT(S)

CONNECT to God's Word

"Let us discern for ourselves what is right; let us learn together what is good." —Job 34:4

- What does this verse mean in your relationship with students' parents?

- In what ways will you try to learn from parents? help them grow their children's faith?

Write a response and prayer to God here...

TO THE POINT

- Parents are allies, not enemies.
- Learn from your students' families and backgrounds.
- Encourage parents to be a part of what you're doing with their teenagers.

TRY IT

Here's a sample letter that one of my volunteers wrote. Use it as a starting point to build a relationship with your students' parents.

Dear Parents,

Welcome to my small group! My name is Alicia, and I've been working with junior high girls for over eight years. I'm married to Phil, and we have a two-year-old daughter named Avery. I have a huge heart for girls your daughter's age! My heart and my hope for your daughter this year is that she would take a next spiritual step in her walk with God. I'm excited to see her grow, learn, laugh, have fun, and ultimately fall into a deeper love relationship with Christ.

One of my goals this year is not only to minister to your daughter but to get to know you and your family, as well. I would love to support you in any way I can. I am committed to communicating with you and faithfully praying for your family. Here are a few questions to help me get to know you better. If you could think about them and then e-mail your answers to me, that would be great. Thanks! Looking forward to a great year!

What is your favorite family tradition?

What qualities stand out in your daughter?

How can I be praying for your family?

What is one spiritual next step you would like to see your daughter take?

MAKE IT PERSONAL

BE AVAILABLE

from Doug Fields

FOR STARTERS

Think of a few people in your life who are always "available" to you.

How often do you contact them with your needs?

What does their availability mean to you?

IN THE TRENCHES

One night at 10:00 someone knocked on our door. This was unusual for us, but we go to bed late so we were still awake. I opened the door to see Kirsten standing there crying.

Before I could say anything, she blurted out, "I just crashed my car! It's up on the sidewalk. I didn't hit anyone, but my mobile phone isn't working, and even though it was a mile walk, I knew I could come to your house and use the phone to call my mom."

Kirsten had only been to our house once before this night, but she knew we were available if she was ever in a crisis.

Who are the Kirstens in your ministry?

TRAINING on the GO

In life, we rarely face *real* emergencies, but when the time arrives, we know that through a quick dial (911) we'll find immediate help. This same emergency principle should be true in youth ministry; it's essential for teenagers to know that a caring adult will be there when a storm comes so they don't have to weather it alone.

Here are a few ways to be available for teenagers (and their parents).

Being available means communicating their importance. Communicate with your students about your role in their lives. Let them know you're happy to be there for them if they are going through something difficult. Let them know that no matter what the emergency is, you're available to talk. I've found that not all students take me up on the offer, but they appreciate the fact that I'm available if the need arises.

Being available means being consistent. Show up regularly to your youth ministry times; a consistent presence communicates your priorities. And if you can, occasionally show up to teenagers' worlds outside of youth ministry; this shows that you really care about what's happening in their lives.

Being available means serving parents. Since there are no perfect handbooks for parenting teenagers, parents need more help than you might imagine. Often, all they need is someone who understands teenagers and is willing to listen. Let parents know they can call you and that you'll listen and offer insight and prayer. If nothing else, you might guide a parent toward another parent with a similar situation.

Being available means setting limits. If you make yourself available, you'll also have to establish boundaries. It's unrealistic to be available to parents and students every moment of every day. Protect your own personal and family time; be there for students and parents when they need you, but don't sacrifice what matters most to you.

Being available means referring. While it's important to be available, it's equally important that you let people know you're not equipped to handle all situations and that you might sometimes need to call for help (such as with abuse, suicide threats, and so on). I'm fairly educated (Bible college and seminary), and yet I'm not trained to deal with all of the crises I've encountered in youth ministry. I've learned to refer to the pros.

If you find yourself in a situation that's too major for you to handle alone, please ask for help. You're not a failure when you do this. Actually, you're a big help. Offer people prayer, encouragement, and support as they find the appropriate help.

The bottom line is, let parents and students know you're available to them when they are in need. Chances are they'll not only ask for your help once in a while but feel encouraged and supported, as well.

BE AVAILABLE

CONNECT to God's Word

"Dear friends, let us love one another, for love comes from God. Everyone who loves has been born of God and knows God." —1 John 4:7

- How does a deeper relationship with God increase your ability to love students?

- How would you measure your availability to teenagers? In what ways should you be more available? What limits might you need to set?

Write a response and prayer to God here...

MAKE IT PERSONAL

TO THE POINT

- Let students know you're available in their crises.
- Availability does not mean you are on call 24/7.
- Don't be afraid to refer to others who are better equipped to help.

TRY IT

Think of three places in your community that are open 24 hours a day—for example, a fast-food restaurant, a market, or a Laundromat. How often do you go to these places? How often do you need them to be open between 10 p.m. and 5 a.m.? How many times have you been so desperate that you couldn't wait until more common hours? As you consider this, think about the message you send to parents and students when you tell them you're available when they have major needs in their life.

With this in mind, consider making a refrigerator magnet like the ones for 24-hour pizza delivery, a doctor's emergency line, plumbing help, or the local real estate agent. These are easy to make: Go to any office supply store and buy adhesive magnets. On a piece of paper, card stock, or cardboard, put your name, information, a funny picture of yourself, and a tag line such as, "Don't be afraid to call when you're hurting." Give this specialized magnet to parents and students to let them know that you care about them and are available.

BE FAMILY-FRIENDLY

from Doug Fields

FOR STARTERS

What were a few of the basic household rules and values during your teenage years?

What were your parents strict about, and what were they more relaxed about?

IN THE TRENCHES

Josh was a film buff; he would see any and every movie that was released. Josh was also a leader of eighth-grade guys in our ministry and often took students to the movies with him. Josh found this difficult with one of his students because this boy wasn't allowed to see anything that didn't have a G rating (and G-rated movies are rare these days).

Needless to say, most of Josh's movie outings included all but one student. The boy was simply following his parents' rules (which was a good thing), but he felt left out because he couldn't be involved in the movie excursions. Josh believed he was respecting the family's rules by not inviting this student; he didn't realize he was hurting the boy's feelings.

Fortunately, Josh eventually decided that for the health and depth of the small group, it was more beneficial to choose activities in which everyone could participate. Josh now goes to the movies with his adult friends rather than students.

How are you like or unlike Josh?

TRAINING on the GO

Sometimes unity in the church seems even more difficult than unity among perfect strangers. However, God created differences in people not so life and ministry would be more difficult but so that we would—through the incredible variety of personalities, gifts, and interests—be able to discover more of the intricacy and elaborateness of the God who created us.

These differences take yet another form when it comes to the families in your youth ministry. Each student and family you work with has different household rules and family values. It's not unusual to find that what's allowed in one home is strictly forbidden in another home. Being sensitive to unique family values will increase your effectiveness as a youth leader.

Developing this kind of sensitivity can be difficult because families have different ideas when it comes to moral and social values. These may range from the types of movies students watch to the appropriate age for dating. Simply put, parents have different ideas about what's best for their children.

As a youth leader, one of your roles is to understand where each family stands on certain issues so you can try to complement what's happening in the students' homes. You might not agree with some of the standards parents set for their teenagers, but it's not your role to judge or disregard a family's value system. It *is* your role to model a Christ-like life, point students toward biblical living, and encourage students to obey their parents. Avoid ever being a divisive force between parent and teenager. (Note: The only exception to this would be when a parent's values collide with God's Word and are harmful or illegal.)

Consider this list of some of the moral and social issues families face:

- age for dating
- use of language or slang
- views on dating, premarital sex, and cohabitation
- approved movies and books
- respect for rules and authority
- alcohol and tobacco use
- money

Pay attention to, and respect, the household rules of the students you work with. For example, if you have a student who needs to be home before 10 o'clock, don't plan activities that break that curfew. Or if your students need to finish schoolwork or chores before they come to youth group, help parents by holding students accountable.

You won't be able to know every rule for every student's household, but you can be aware of what's important to each family. The idea here is to send a strong message that you care deeply about families. You also want teenagers to hear that you support their parents and won't contradict their values.

When you're with parents, let them know you're on board with what they're trying to do with their teenagers—and you want to help them by being an advocate for their values and decisions.

BE FAMILY-FRIENDLY

CONNECT to God's Word

"There is one body and one Spirit—just as you were called to one hope when you were called."
—Ephesians 4:4

- Think of parents who seem completely different from you. How can you support their values?

- What commitment will you make to unify your students, despite their different backgrounds?

Write a response and prayer to God here...

TO THE POINT

- Recognize that each family has its own set of values.

- Understand, support, and respect parents.

- Accept each student and family where they are and minister to them accordingly.

TRY IT

When we're watching TV, we don't always pay close attention to the family dynamics being portrayed. The same might be true in our youth ministries. When we're with students, we don't always consider their family dynamics. Try this TV-watching experiment to help you dig into your students' family situations.

Watch two TV shows that depict different types of families and that represent different values. Consider the characteristics of the parental figures. What are the relationships like between all of the family members? What type of environment do they live in? How do the siblings interact with one another? What values stand out within each family? What things are not allowed, and what things are "no big deal" in each family?

Then, think of the students you work with, and go through these same questions for each of their families. How will the answers affect your ministry to these teenagers? If you don't know the answers, what will you do to find out?

MAKE IT PERSONAL

LEARN FROM YOUTH CULTURE

from Doug Fields

FOR STARTERS

What was youth culture like when you were in junior high and high school?

What was popular with you and your friends?

What were the current trends?

IN THE TRENCHES

Jeremiah, a veteran volunteer, was preparing a Sunday school lesson on relationships and dating for his tenth-graders. In order to write discussion questions geared for his students, he wanted to better understand where his students were coming from on this topic. What were current views on dating and relationships? Were they seeing any healthy, biblical examples? What messages were they picking up from their culture?

So he began interviewing students, asking questions such as, "Where do you go to learn about dating and relationships?" "Whose advice do you seek when you are dating someone?" "Who is someone you believe has a perfect relationship?"

The results weren't too surprising: He found that most students' perspectives were in great part shaped by the media, the Internet, and their friends. This was a helpful exercise because Jeremiah needed help creating a context for the relevance of God's Word to issues in their lives. He didn't rest on what he already knew; therefore, he was able to connect with students on a more personal and deeper level.

How do you (or can you) carry out Jeremiah's type of investigation?

TRAINING on the GO

Recently I connected with a 40-something youth leader who had recently gotten a tattoo and had his ears pierced. I asked him what had inspired his new look, and he confidently answered, "Just trying to reach youth!" He was so proud to say that—and I was so stunned to hear it. Being relevant to teenagers and their culture doesn't require being pierced with a needle or stabbed with ink.

However, I do believe it's important for youth leaders to make some attempts to know about teenage culture and understand what's happening in the teenage world.

You don't need to embrace their culture, and you definitely don't need to *become* it. You just need to know what's influencing them. Teenagers appreciate it when you seek to understand them; your relationships with them will create the relevance you need. I've never met a teenager who said, "Doug, I wish you dressed like me and listened to my music and hung out where I hang out."

Your best resource for learning about student culture is *your students*. By peeking into their lives and culture, you can learn what influences their lives and impacts their faith. However, when students trust you enough to let you into their world, be careful not to destroy that trust by using their culture as a weapon against them. For instance, if a student watches a TV show you don't approve of, resist condemnation. Instead, ask questions such as, "What stands out about this show?" or "Why do you watch this show every week?" Look for good conversations and teachable moments as you learn from students.

Learn about what influences your students. Find ways to get inside students' culture. Begin by asking some of the following basic questions:

- What TV shows and movies do you watch?
- What Web sites do you and your friends visit?
- What magazines or books do you read?
- What do you like to do for fun?
- What are your favorite songs and types of music?

Take what they tell you, and begin your own investigation. You don't need to watch an entire movie or read an entire issue of a favorite magazine to understand everything. You're just looking for a small taste of what's influencing them. Take note of magazine headlines; check out the themes of the TV shows; spend five minutes poking around a favorite Web site.

Allow culture to motivate you. Once you get a glimpse of what students spend time with, you can look for opportunities to ask specific questions and challenge them toward a next level in their faith. Take what you're learning and connect it to your ministry to them.

When you get to know their culture, your ministry can become more relevant to their needs. Making references to their culture when you teach or talk to students can deepen their faith journey and draw them closer to God.

LEARN FROM YOUTH CULTURE

CONNECT to God's Word

"Now this is our boast: Our conscience testifies that we have conducted ourselves in the world, and especially in our relations with you, in the holiness and sincerity that are from God. We have done so not according to worldly wisdom but according to God's grace." —2 Corinthians 1:12

- According to this verse, how can we conduct ourselves *in the world* but still with holiness and sincerity from God?
- What do you suppose "worldly wisdom" is?

Write a response and prayer to God here...

TO THE POINT

- You don't have to embrace or live youth culture—just seek to understand it.
- Ask students questions about their culture.
- Don't be afraid to challenge students to think about how culture impacts their faith.

TRY IT

Here are some ways to stay connected to student culture without immersing yourself in it.

Daily dose. Set the opening page of your Internet browser to current events and youth culture news (two examples are www.cpyu.org and www.youthministry.com).

Weekly dose. While you're in the grocery store, flip through a magazine that's popular with students. You don't need to read all the articles, but look at headlines and photos to get insight into the things students are reading and topics that might be influencing them.

Monthly dose. Watch a TV program your students like. Great discussions might be had from what you see.

Use some of what you learn to help with a teaching or Bible study. Or insert something relevant into a conversation with a student and see what response you get. The more you understand, the more you can connect teenagers to what should be their ultimate influence—a personal relationship with Jesus.

MAKE IT PERSONAL

POINT TO CHRIST IN CULTURE

from Doug Fields

FOR STARTERS

In what ways do you see Jesus in current culture? movies? music? trends?

Have you ever talked to teenagers about their culture? Why or why not?

IN THE TRENCHES

I knew a veteran volunteer named Ron who used culture to his advantage. He led a group of boys, mentoring them through all four years of high school.

One of the ways he would connect with his guys was through a weekly e-mail, to which he would attach an article, quote, verse, or video clip. He sent the guys anything that was meaningful to him and revealed something about a relationship with Jesus.

Not only were the boys hearing from him every week—they were also given something to spark spiritual thought. Ron was always on the lookout for anything that might interest his guys and connect them to Jesus. How are you like or unlike Ron?

TRAINING on the GO

I often experience a deep sense of God's truth and the beauty of his character through the story line of a movie or the notes of a song. If you can too, you can give teenagers a gift by helping them experience the same.

Your students are exposed to messages about Jesus outside of church through current events and culture. They see images of Jesus on secular magazine covers and as a marketing image through clothing lines. They hear about him in youth music and videos (both secular and sacred). Basically, culture doesn't shy away from Jesus—even if it doesn't often acknowledge him as the Messiah and Savior.

You have countless opportunities to use culture to point teenagers to Jesus. Let me give you a few ideas.

Read the headlines. Read the newspaper, pick up a magazine, or scan daily headlines on the Internet. You would be surprised by how many articles are about Jesus; save the articles for students to read, use them in your teachings, or use the headlines to prompt discussion. You might even e-mail articles to students to show them that Jesus is being discussed everywhere.

Look for media specials. Every year (especially around Christmas and Easter) several television specials or movies focus on the life of Jesus. Choose one of these shows and, the week before it airs, ask students to watch it. Then use the show to spark conversation.

Search the Internet. The Internet is full of articles, essays, and personal blogs that can help point your students to Jesus. With a few key search words and a couple of mouse clicks, you'll have access to a mountain of available information.

Few scholars deny the existence of Jesus Christ, but many deny his divinity (his claim to be God). I know several Christians who have made faith commitments to Jesus as their Savior by taking the time to explore answers to their questions. Today's culture is filled with rich treasures and meaningful information that you can mine to help lead teenagers to transformed lives.

POINT TO CHRIST IN CULTURE

CONNECT to God's Word

"For since the creation of the world God's invisible qualities—his eternal power and divine nature—have been clearly seen, being understood from what has been made, so that men are without excuse." —Romans 1:20

- When was the last time you experienced God in a real way? How can you link this to your ministry to students?
- What will you do to connect Christ to your students' culture so they better understand God's character?

Write a response and prayer to God here...

TO THE POINT

- Be on the lookout for Christ in culture.
- Don't be afraid to use culture as a tool to minister to your students.

TRY IT

Choose a topic you know will be relevant to your students and will trigger their interest, such as dating, friendships, family relationships, temptation, and so on. Then find something in culture that relates to this topic and will ultimately lead students back to Jesus. For example, if you choose friendship, you might find a popular Web site that emphasizes friendships; interactive online communities are all about connecting people to one another. Use the Web site as a cultural tool to explore the body of Christ—we are all created to be connected to one another.

Here are some other ideas for using culture in your ministry times.

- Play a song that has lyrics relating to what you're teaching or discussing.
- Show a movie clip that illustrates a point or students' questions.
- Discuss the strategy and elements of video-game play, and talk about the spiritual connects.

Through cultural tools, help students learn to find Jesus in the things they're already looking at.

MAKE IT PERSONAL

RECOGNIZE THEIR REALITIES

from Doug Fields

FOR STARTERS

What did you once believe was real that you now know isn't?

What do you think are the biggest differences between what we see in movies or on TV and what happens in real life?

IN THE TRENCHES

Caleb is a student in our ministry who comes from a very wealthy family. He's involved with our youth ministry on a regular basis, but he hasn't yet committed to a relationship with Jesus and decided to follow God's ways. Caleb feels like he doesn't need Christ because his life is filled with lots of possessions. That's his real-life culture. Although Caleb actually does *want* for something, he just can't seem to define it.

What he does need in his life is someone to help him move beyond what he has and see what he doesn't have—a relationship with Jesus. Caleb needs a friend to show him that the culture that's influencing him is shallow and won't provide what he really wants. Thankfully, when the time is right, he'll have in his small-group leader all he needs—wise counsel, acceptance, friendship, and an example of authentic faith.

Who are the Calebs in your ministry?

TRAINING on the GO

Teenagers are daily immersed in a combination of their pop culture (for example, music, movies, and the Internet) and their life culture (for example, school, family, and friends). One of your roles, as a volunteer, is to help students navigate *real culture*—the one they live in. You do this by building healthy relationships, helping them make good decisions, and guiding them toward Jesus.

To understand more about your students' culture, you need to begin with their daily lives. What type of everyday culture surrounds your students? What are their home lives like? What are their schools like? What's their family and financial situation? Who are their friends? Aside from what they watch and what they listen to, what influences your students on a daily basis? What makes up *their* culture?

When you take time to better understand teenagers' world, you'll be a wiser and more valuable youth volunteer. You can begin to help them recognize the positives and negatives of their culture.

Point out the positive. Help students see their good cultural influences. Not everything is negative. I've found teenagers to be surprised and amazed when a caring Christian adult sees something positive in their culture and comments on it.

As I write this, online social networks are skyrocketing in popularity, connecting millions of teenagers. I readily admit there is a downside to these kinds of Web sites. Using them has some dangers, but there are positives as well. I see in these kinds of communities an acknowledgment of the need for relationships and a place where teenagers can openly express themselves to friends who really care about them. When I choose to point out these types of positive things, students are much more open to hearing my opinion on the negatives as well. This opens up rich dialogue that connects to discussion about friendships in the body of Christ.

Identify the negative. Just as you help students understand positive elements of youth culture, you also point out the negatives, with the goal of helping them understand the possible effects. When I do this, I try hard not to appear judgmental or overbearing, but I'm also not afraid to offer guidance when I see something in students' culture that could lead them astray. Students might very well resist your guidance, but at least they'll know you care enough to speak up. When you are bold in addressing unhealthy habits, relationships, and activities, you have an opportunity to nudge students toward wise spiritual decisions.

At times it can be difficult to watch students navigate their real culture. Sometimes they make good choices, and sometimes they are so far off track you're not sure they'll make it back. But youth ministry is about helping teenagers navigate the journey, and it's a marathon, not a sprint. Take time to understand where they're coming from, and speak truth in love for all parts of culture.

RECOGNIZE THEIR REALITIES

CONNECT to God's Word

"Be very careful, then, how you live—not as unwise but as wise, making the most of every opportunity, because the days are evil."—Ephesians 5:15-16

Wise living does not necessarily mean avoiding everything that is "worldly." Wisdom is found in those who choose to live like Christ in spite of and even in the midst of evil.

- In what ways can you "make the most of every opportunity" in your life and ministry?
- How will you help your students navigate both the positive and negative elements of their culture?

Write a response and prayer to God here...

TO THE POINT

- Understand the real culture your students live in.
- Help students identify both the positives and negatives of their culture.
- Be there for your students through the good and the bad choices.

TRY IT

Meet your students at a store that has items teenagers use in their everyday lives (for example, a department store, a music store, a clothing store, a computer store). You can do this with students individually or as a group. Give your students 20 minutes to find three items that symbolize their life or culture.

If you don't want them to carry the items (because you'll have to return them to the appropriate place later), have them write the name of the item so they can share later. When the time is up, meet up again and have everyone explain each of the items and why it was selected. Ask students to share why the items represent who they are and what their life is like. Next, have each student brainstorm one word that connects to each item and reveals an emotion; for instance, *comforting, fun,* and so on.

Afterward, think of ways to encourage each student to a deeper relationship with God, based on what you learned about their personal desires.

MAKE IT PERSONAL

DEFINE THE CULTURE OF YOUR MINISTRY
from Doug Fields

FOR STARTERS

In what ways do you think you're currently influencing your students?

What words would you use to describe the ministry culture you've set?

IN THE TRENCHES

Linda was a volunteer who was very passionate about loving other volunteer leaders; she was extremely gifted in the areas of encouragement and hospitality. Before I met Linda, my volunteer staff meetings were good but not great. Linda saw the potential and started using her God-given gifts to make these meetings better.

She took the lead in the planning, the food, the decorations—even making fun awards for other volunteers. She helped make a fun and creative atmosphere that communicated to our volunteers that they were loved and appreciated.

After just a few meetings, Linda had changed our volunteer culture. My volunteers quickly adapted to this new culture and now actively contribute to it. All it took to change the culture of our volunteer team was a woman willing to use her gifts and express her passion.

How are you like or unlike Linda?

TRAINING on the GO

Youth ministries create their own cultures by what they value—and what they don't value. You might hear someone say, "We have a very encouraging culture." Or you may hear, "Our culture is very friendly to nonchurched students." The longer you serve in youth ministry, the more opportunities you'll have to contribute to the existing culture of the ministry. I want my volunteers to know that they can either contribute to an existing culture or use their passion and gifts to create new values within the culture.

If you don't know the values in your youth ministry culture, ask your pastor or lead youth worker. And if the values aren't defined, you might offer to help brainstorm about them with other leaders. But even without defined values, real actions provide evidence for a healthy youth ministry—even if the values are not openly articulated.

Here are three actions all youth volunteers should take to create a spiritually thriving culture for students.

Set spiritual goals with your students. Think through where you would like to help lead your students spiritually. What is God teaching them? What Scriptures are essential to growing their faith? Take some time to establish what you believe will have the most impact on each student in an individual relationship with God. Be the type of leader who is constantly encouraging students toward next steps that will contribute to spiritual deepening.

Make traditions with your students. Look for opportunities to create yearly, monthly, or weekly traditions that will become memorable for students. For example, one of our volunteer leaders opens her small-group time by reading the same Bible verse each week. Another leader and his students serve at a homeless shelter on every major holiday, and another leader hosts a monthly spaghetti dinner for her small-group girls. These traditions communicate that students are special and valuable and contribute to creating a positive culture in your ministry.

Create memories with your students. Traditions are a great way to create memories, but memories can be anything from ongoing events to one-time experiences—anything that students will never forget. When my family eats together, we always recall and laugh about fun memories; it's amazing how memories create a strong relational bond. By creating memories with your teenagers, you'll add that element of "family" to your ministry. Taking trips together, sharing meals, or just hanging out can create memories and help shape a healthy, vibrant culture.

DEFINE THE CULTURE OF YOUR MINISTRY

CONNECT to God's Word

"My purpose is that they may be encouraged in heart and united in love, so that they may have the full riches of complete understanding, in order that they may know the mystery of God, namely, Christ, in whom are hidden all the treasures of wisdom and knowledge." —Colossians 2:2-3

- In which one or two areas are you most passionate and gifted? How can these areas have a positive impact on the youth ministry?
- In what ways will you actively create a spiritually thriving culture with students?

Write a response and prayer to God here...

TO THE POINT

- Examine your current youth ministry influence.
- Define personal actions that contribute to your youth ministry culture.

TRY IT

Choose one of these three actions, and then act on it.

Set spiritual goals. Give each student in your group an envelope and a piece of paper. Ask students to put their names on the envelope and then write three spiritual goals for themselves on the paper. Take their papers and envelopes, and add three additional spiritual goals or next steps that you would like to see them take. Seal the envelopes and put them away for a semester. At that time, open the envelopes with the students and discuss what has happened.

Make traditions. Choose a certain day of the month for your small-group members to focus on affirming each other. Help students go a little deeper than surface admiration or praise and encourage one another's character, giving specific examples. Chances are it will become something your students will look forward to each month.

Create memories. Take photos of your students throughout the year, and then create a collage for them. Frame it and have students sign one another's frames.

MAKE IT PERSONAL

STAY IN IT FOR THE LONG HAUL

from Doug Fields

FOR STARTERS

What's the longest trip you've ever taken?

What were some of the difficulties you experienced along the way?

Did you ever feel like quitting the trip early? Why or why not?

IN THE TRENCHES

Gary has been a volunteer with our junior high students for more than 15 years. Because Gary loves his role and has been very faithful and consistent over the years, he's well known by students, other volunteers, and parents. Every Sunday morning, someone is looking for Gary because he is one of the most familiar faces in our youth ministry. Parents come to say hello, students from years past stop in to catch up, and other volunteers look to him for guidance. He has had an incredible impact in the lives of students and on our church family. What makes Gary special is his willingness to love students week in and week out—year after year—and soon, decade after decade.

How can Gary's story encourage you?

TRAINING on the GO

Youth ministry can be very tough at times! But if you want to experience the reward of watching young lives transformed, committing to teenagers for the long haul is the way to see this happen. One of my life goals is to help youth leaders understand that the longer they remain in youth ministry, the more opportunities they'll have to impact the lives of students—and the easier youth ministry becomes. Read this carefully: Youth ministry isn't easy, but it does get easier over the long haul.

Each year that you give to teenagers will result in greater impact and influence. One of the reasons longevity is important is because teenagers already have enough short-term adults moving in and out of their lives; they don't need more at church. Teenagers need consistent adults who will commit to them through the different stages of growth and who will stick around during the good and bad times of adolescence.

Anyone can look good from a distance and for a short period of time, but longevity gives students an opportunity to watch you through your ups and downs. As you share life with students, you'll expose them to parts of your personal spiritual journey and your decision-making process. It's powerful for teenagers to see your faith in action on a consistent basis and over a long period of time.

In addition to allowing students to see your long-term faith, you'll be around for more of *their* life events. If you last in ministry, you'll help celebrate first jobs, cheer students on as they pass their driver's test, smile proudly at graduations, counsel them on their dating relationships—and you may be involved in their weddings.

Why do I want you to imagine the future? Because the longer you're in students' lives, the better your relationship will be. I've been in youth ministry for over 25 years, and I've seen a number of my students graduate from college, get married, and have children of their own. It has also been a blessing to watch them follow Jesus and teach their own families to follow Jesus. Seeing that encourages me to stay in youth ministry for another year. Experiencing life with teenagers over the long haul will allow you to reap the rewards of the seeds you plant in their hearts now.

STAY IN IT FOR THE LONG HAUL

CONNECT to God's Word

"Then Abraham waited patiently, and he received what God had promised."
—Hebrews 6:15, New Living Translation

- What's something you've been waiting to see happen in your ministry?
- How can you stay faithful for the long haul? What might be getting in the way of your ministry longevity?

Write a response and prayer to God here...

TO THE POINT

- Relationships take time.
- Good youth ministry is long-term youth ministry.
- Don't be a short-term adult in the lives of your students.

TRY IT

Pretend that you are going to Antarctica—yes, Antarctica. It's the farthest and most exotic place I can think of. It would be a "long haul" to get there. Think for a moment: How much preparation would go into planning a trip like that? How long would it take to get there? What would be your means of transportation? Would you go alone? What would it cost? Go online and chart a course to your destination.

As you consider this fictitious trip, think about how much goes into planning a trip like this. But also consider that the more time and energy you put into the front of the trip, the more rewarding it will be. The same principle is true in your ministry to students. The more time you put into the relationships with students and your youth ministry, the more rewarding ministry will be for you.

MAKE IT PERSONAL

SET THE PACE

from Doug Fields

FOR STARTERS

If you consider your time to be overextended, what do you think is the root cause? Or if you have a lot of wasted time, what's something practical you could add to your life?

IN THE TRENCHES

Sometimes the best intentions can burn you out in youth ministry. Jim was a very energetic and enthusiastic volunteer leader; he joined our team in September as a small-group leader. He was a single guy who made a living as a fireman; with this job, he had a lot of time on his hands because he would work three or four 24-hour shifts and have the rest of the week off.

His flexible schedule allowed him to jump into our ministry activities with both feet. He really loved being involved with students and soon added more to his original commitment of leading a small group. Jim began volunteering in our Sunday morning program and attending our camps and monthly activities.

Jim's struggle was that he really loved serving in the youth ministry but found himself having no personal life outside of his ministry to teenagers. By the end of the school year, he was finished. He had poured himself so intensely into teenagers that he hadn't set a realistic pace for his ministry. Simply put, he burned out. Jim took some time off from our youth ministry and returned a year later. The second time around, he started with fewer commitments, an understanding of reality, and a different pace. We thank God he's still serving in our ministry today.

How are you like or unlike Jim?

TRAINING on the GO

Burnout is a very real danger for youth ministry volunteers. Because I want you to last in youth ministry, here are some principles that will help you set a healthy pace for your ministry to students.

Pacesetter 1: Alone time with God. There's no way around this one. You *must* spend intimate time with God if you're going to last in ministry. Ministering to students can be draining and overwhelming; refreshing your soul is essential to keep ministry from feeling overwhelming. My prediction is that you will last in youth ministry for the long term if you make it a priority to spend frequent time with God, surrendering your heart and ministry to him. A growing relationship with God is essential to being an effective youth leader.

Pacesetter 2: Evaluation of your commitment. Please understand that your pace in youth ministry does not always need to be at top speed. For example, you might have a difficult semester in college, your job might be very demanding during the summer, or you might experience a crisis with your family that requires full attention. When you consistently evaluate your life and time needs, you'll experience naturally slow and full-throttle seasons (and everything in between) in ministry.

During the last 25 years, my wife has mastered the juggling of seasons in her youth ministry commitment. Some seasons she had more time freedom and could take on additional responsibilities, and other seasons she was too busy and had to back off. But whether seasons are busy or slow, she's committed to being involved over the long haul. She understands that to last in ministry, she must continually evaluate what her role looks like.

Don't be afraid to give up ministry when your personal life needs you to. Youth ministry will be around through all of those seasons, so have the freedom to step out every once in a while to get recharged or focus on what's important.

Pacesetter 3: Mixing it up. Don't be afraid to mix it up every once in a while. I love it when volunteers want to try some new things in our youth ministry; changes keep long-haul ministry experiences fresh, intriguing, and meaningful. For example, if you're a small-group leader, lead your students in an activity you've never done before. Or if you teach on a regular basis, try a totally different teaching style. Try to make variety a part of your ministry.

It's vital that you take a look at the pace you're keeping in ministry. I have seen so many youth leaders burn out over the years because they run at too furious a pace. Spend personal, quality time with God; look closely at your commitments; and mix things up to keep your ministry fresh.

SET THE PACE

CONNECT to God's Word

"If you find honey, eat just enough—too much of it, and you will vomit." —Proverbs 25:16

- How is your ministry to teenagers like or unlike honey? How can you prevent yourself from getting "sick" because of your ministry pace?

- What will you make a fresh commitment to—alone time with God, evaluating commitments, or mixing it up? Why and how?

Write a response and prayer to God here…

TO THE POINT

- Spend time with God to stay refreshed.
- Evaluate your commitments, and readjust to prevent burnout.
- Mix it up to keep ministry fresh.

TRY IT

Set your watch or a timer for two minutes. You have these few minutes to complete all of the following tasks (no cheating):

- Read one e-mail.
- Get a drink of water.
- Say hello to someone (for example, a classmate, a co-worker, a child).
- Jog in place for 20 seconds.
- Write someone a note.
- Call a friend to catch up.
- Do one push-up.

Did you complete all of the tasks? Did you even come close? Sometimes in youth ministry we're faced with an impossible pace. Chances are you looked at the list and did what you *could* accomplish in the time allotted. The same is true in ministry: You need to look at your priorities in your ministry and then set a realistic and maintainable pace.

MAKE IT PERSONAL

MATURE IN MINISTRY

from Doug Fields

▶ FOR STARTERS

Think of yourself in your younger life stages, such as elementary school, junior high, high school, and so on. What were you like in each of these stages? What have been the most significant growth areas of your life?

IN THE TRENCHES

Youth leaders do get better with age. The other day, I was sitting with one of my longtime volunteers, Matt, who was telling me a story about something he did early in youth ministry. The story went something like this:

I was 21 and a volunteer at my church in northern California. For my first ministry experience, I was teamed up with ninth-grade guys. I worked overtime to get these kids to think I was cool. I tried so hard to be their friend, hoping that I could teach them something about God along the way. In fact, I believed that the cooler they thought I was, the more open they would be to growing spiritually.

Anyway, one afternoon I decided to let the boys take turns driving my car. I know—it was stupid. Not one of my students had a driver's license, but I thought they would think I was cool for allowing them to drive my car. And they did—until one of them crashed it into a light pole.

That started a maturing process for me. Over the next four years, I learned that they couldn't care less about how cool I was. They wanted a leader. They were looking for someone who was growing spiritually and real in his faith. The car crash made me realize that I'm in youth ministry not to be a peer, but to be a loving adult who points teenagers to Jesus Christ."

What connections can you make from Matt's story to your ministry?

TRAINING on the GO

The first few years of youth ministry for a volunteer are often the most difficult years. If you're a veteran youth leader, you know what I'm talking about; if you're a rookie, believe me, it'll keep getting easier. Even as a longtime youth leader, I'm still making mistakes. But the longer you're in ministry, the more you'll mature, grow, and learn.

No one begins youth ministry with all the right skills in place. Every youth leader needs to develop new skills—and that's one of the reasons you're reading this. Maturing in youth ministry requires that you be a learner. It also requires that you be willing to grow through failures and successes.

Thank you for your commitment to learn—and thank you for allowing me to challenge you with two ways to mature in ministry.

Learn with humility. You don't need to be the Superman or Wonder Woman of ministry, able to leap tall student problems with a single bound, faster than the speeding mouth of the sarcastic, deflecting the bullets of criticism off your chest—you get the picture. You're not perfect and you don't know everything. The good news is, you don't have to act like you do. Be humble enough to learn from God and from others.

Learn from everything. No matter what youth ministry throws at you—good, bad, or ugly—learn from it. I realize it's difficult to think about valuable lessons coming from dumb ministry mistakes, but I genuinely believe that every ministry experience can shape you to be more effective. Your successes will become traditions, and your failures will become giant warning signs. Learning doesn't just "happen"; the only way you can learn from your experiences is by taking time to stop and think about them. For example, for two years, I had a long drive home from my small group. I made a commitment to a quiet ride home—not listening to music or talking to anyone. It was a great time to think about what I'd learned that night—although the drive was terrible after some of the really bad small-group times! Take hold of what you learn, and talk with another leader about it.

Don't be afraid to grow old. I began youth ministry when I was 18 years old. Today, I'm embarrassed to think about some of the things I did and said during those early years. Writing this over 25 years later, I can say with certainty that I am a better youth leader; as I've aged and matured, my ministry skills have matured as well. I have grown in wisdom, decision making, and relationships. And so will you. Remember: Learn, make mistakes, celebrate victories, grow old, and give it time—lots and lots of time.

MATURE IN MINISTRY

CONNECT to God's Word

"Praise be to the name of God for ever and ever; wisdom and power are his. He changes times and seasons; he sets up kings and deposes them. He gives wisdom to the wise and knowledge to the discerning. He reveals deep and hidden things; he knows what lies in darkness, and light dwells with him." —Daniel 2:20-22

- How has God already matured you in ministry? How are you looking to mature in the future?

- In what ways will you praise God through learning and growing in ministry? How will this impact students?

Write a response and prayer to God here…

TO THE POINT

- Maturing in ministry takes time.
- Practice humility and be willing to learn.

TRY IT

If you don't already, start keeping a ministry journal. Take time to document how you're learning and growing. Note key events, experiences, and moments. Spend time writing about students' milestones and spiritual growth, what you're enjoying, and what you're struggling with. Record your mistakes and "bloopers," as well as the lessons and changes that come out of those mistakes. A ministry journal will not only give you something to learn from in the future but serve as great snapshot of your ministry and teachings for others to learn from.

MAKE IT PERSONAL

STEP DOWN GRACIOUSLY

from Doug Fields

FOR STARTERS

What emotions have you felt when you've left something behind? Excitement? Fear? Loss? Relief? Disappointment?

IN THE TRENCHES

Brian, a volunteer in our youth ministry, came into my office one day and told me his time in youth ministry was coming to an end. Immediately, my heart was heavy with disappointment because Brian was an incredible volunteer. He told me that his own children were growing up and that he needed to be home more to be their "shepherd" (a term we use for our youth volunteers).

Brian loved working with teenagers, but he felt that God was leading him to do a Bible study and go on fun outings with his two sons. He told me he loved our ministry and would be praying for us—but it was time to begin focusing somewhere else. I was really sad to see Brian end his run in our youth ministry, but he was definitely following what God wanted for him. Sometimes great ministry leaders need to step away.

TRAINING on the GO

It's my prayer that your passion for students will last until you're physically unable to do youth ministry. However, that isn't a reality for everyone. There comes a time for every youth leader to exit. Regardless of whether you feel called to stop, can't serve anymore, or don't want to serve anymore—the key is knowing how to step out of youth ministry in the best way possible.

Now, if you're new to working with teenagers, I hope the idea of stopping sounds crazy to you because you can't even imagine leaving youth ministry. However, no matter what stage you're in, it's important to think about how you will pass the torch and leave youth ministry in a healthy and positive way.

Be aware of your heart's condition. Unfortunately, some people stay in youth ministry too long and become disillusioned. To prevent this, regularly check your eagerness to serve with a Christ-centered passion. A volunteer on a healthy youth ministry team needs a heart for students and a heart for God; if this still describes you, then you probably have more time on your youth ministry clock. If you find that you're waning in your level of passion for students (which isn't something to feel guilty about), it might be time to prepare an exit strategy.

Plan to leave on good terms. If you feel you've been wronged by someone in the youth ministry, seek reconciliation before leaving. If you have done something to tarnish the reputation of the youth ministry, please take time to make amends with students, other volunteers, and the lead youth worker. I never want volunteers to leave youth ministry with regrets about relationships and responsibilities.

Your legacy will outlast your departure. When you step down from the youth ministry, your legacy will outlive the hole in the ministry created by your leaving. I'm referring not to a legacy of popularity, but one of eternal impact on young lives. The legacy you leave will continue in the lives and faith of those you touched.

Pass the torch. After years of youth ministry experience, it would be a shame to put that expertise on a shelf and not have others benefit from what you've learned. My hope is that you'll become a mentor to new youth leaders who often feel overwhelmed and undertrained. Before you leave, pass the torch of your knowledge and skill set to a new youth ministry volunteer. Some of my best volunteers are men and women who were mentored by other volunteers God was moving out of youth ministry. If you've served for over two years in youth ministry, you have something to pass on. And if you recognize that you're coming to the end of your service in youth ministry, you'd do a great favor to a leader coming after you by inviting him or her to serve alongside you as you finish out your service (sort of like training an apprentice).

No matter when you depart from youth ministry, please take time to step down in a positive, God-honoring way.

STEP DOWN GRACIOUSLY

CONNECT to God's Word

"There is a time for everything, and a season for every activity under heaven." —Ecclesiastes 3:1

- What season of youth ministry are you in right now? How is your level of passion and excitement?

- How do you sense God leading you in youth ministry, now and in the future? If you feel he's calling you to step down at some point, how will you do it?

Write a response and prayer to God here…

TO THE POINT

- Examine your heart often.
- It's OK to leave youth ministry—just do it right.
- Your ministry will leave a legacy in the lives of others you have invested in.
- Don't leave without replacing yourself with others.

TRY IT

Find a small section of PVC pipe. On one side of the pipe, write a verse that has been significant in your ministry to students. On the other side, write your most worthwhile ministry advice.

Now, find a volunteer leader who is newer to the youth ministry than you, and pass the baton. You can also do this for your students; however, instead of writing youth ministry advice, give them a life thought, encouraging phrase, or an inspirational quote.

Feel free to use this idea even if you're not planning on stepping out of youth ministry anytime soon. This activity is something that can begin to deepen your legacy now in the lives of other leaders and students.

MAKE IT PERSONAL

THEME INDEX

Accountability	26, 49-50, 71-74
Affection	53
Affirmation	39-40, 49-50, 59-60, 105-106
Asking for help	27, 33, 35-36, 45, 47-48, 93-94
Behavior	45, 46, 51-52, 83-84
Being effective	9, 11, 31-32, 37-38
Being understanding	51-52, 85
Boundaries	37-38, 49-50, 93-94
Building relationships	43-44, 51-52, 53-54, 71-72
Burnout	11, 107
Busyness	9, 11
Care for students	79-80, 85-86, 93-94
Confidentiality	65-66, 79-82
Conflict	43, 61-62
Culture	97-104
Discipline	45-46,
Distractions	10, 11, 41-44
Earning trust	70-71, 79-82
Encouragement	39-40, 93-94, 99
Gifts	15, 18, 19, 35-36, 103-104
God's love	9-14
Guiding students' choices	69-75, 83-84, 95-96, 101-102
Humility	27, 31-32, 35-36, 75-75, 110
Innovation	21, 25
Leadership	47
Listening	65-66, 77-78, 85-86
Media messages	33, 96, 99-100
Meeting ministry needs	17, 21-22, 25, 49-50, 105-112
Meeting students' needs	19, 47-48, 51-52, 67-68
Mentoring	27-28, 48, 111
Milestones	59-60, 110
Ministry vision	17, 103
Money	89-90
Parents	29-30, 65-66, 87-96
Passion	9, 15-16, 25
Perception	23, 63-64
Pointing students to God's Word	7, 39-40, 47-48, 69-70, 73-74, 76, 86
Priorities	37-40
Recruiting	19, 23
Relationship with God	9-16, 107-108
Researching adolescence	33-34, 51-52, 97-98
Responsibility	47-48, 63-66
Rest	13-14, 38
Safety	65, 69-70
Setting a Christ-like example	9, 69-72,
Setting goals	25-26, 48, 49-50, 103-104
Spiritual growth	9-10, 12, 14, 26, 39, 104
Teamwork	15, 17-26, 31
Time management	13, 35-44, 87-88, 107
Tough love	47-48, 71-74
Using resources	33-34, 98-100
Values	95

SCRIPTURE INDEX

Leviticus 25:3-5	38
Deuteronomy 5:32-33	42
Job 2:13	86
Job 34:4	92
Psalm 1:1-3	26
Psalm 19:14	24
Psalm 26:2-3	50
Psalm 31:14-16	44
Psalm 46:10	12
Psalm 139:1-4	40
Proverbs 3:11-13	46
Proverbs 4:5-7	30
Proverbs 9:9-10	28
Proverbs 10:12-14	82
Proverbs 12:15	64
Proverbs 16:16	76
Proverbs 17:16	90
Proverbs 25:16	108
Proverbs 27:23	70
Ecclesiastes 1:9-10	84
Ecclesiastes 3:1	112
Ecclesiastes 4:9-10	36
Isaiah 30:15-16	14
Isaiah 55:8-9	20
Jeremiah 17:7	80
Daniel 2:20-22	110
Zephaniah 3:17	60
Luke 6:34-36	52
Luke 10:27	10
Romans 1:20	100
Romans 12:6-9	22
Romans 14:19	62
1 Corinthians 12:7	16
1 Corinthians 13: 4-7	56
1 Corinthians 13:1-3	58
2 Corinthians 1:12	98
Galatians 6:3-5	66
Ephesians 4:4	96
Ephesians 4:16	18
Ephesians 5:15-16	102
Philippians 3:13-14	34
Philippians 3:17	72
Colossians 2:2-3	104
1 Thessalonians 2:8	54
2 Timothy 3:16	74
Hebrews 3:13	68
Hebrews 6:15	106
James 1:19	78
James 5:16	32
1 Peter 1:22-23	48
1 Peter 2:17	88
1 John 4:7	94

E-COURAGEMENT BLAST 1

Each of these E-couragement Blasts is included on the CD-ROM, in both rich text format (RTF) and portable document file (PDF). Feel free to edit these e-couragements to match your ministry and the needs of your volunteers.

You're Human

Brain Food

The most important thing you can do as a youth leader isn't to give the most dynamic talk, to plan the best retreat, or to play the best guitar. The most important thing you do is love God—and focus on your relationship with Jesus. It all starts there.

This kind of love is contagious; it can't be contained. When you love God with everything you are, it oozes into the lives of those around you. Students are particularly observant and will easily pick up on your love for God.

Do this wisely. Pursue God with your mind—seeking truth for the sake of your own faith and for responding to the questions of your students. Be okay with telling them that you don't know all the answers, and work with them to seek truth together. As you're dependent on God, this pursuit of answers will be more natural.

Be encouraged—God is using you to further his kingdom in ways that are beyond your wildest imagination!

Like They Say...

"God's creation was for definite purposes. Humans were intended to know, love, and obey God."

—Millard J. Erickson, *Introducing Christian Doctrine*

God's Word

"Hear, O Israel: The Lord our God, the Lord is one. Love the Lord your God with all your heart and with all your soul and with all your strength. These commandments that I give you today are to be upon your hearts. Impress them on your children. Talk about them when you sit at home and when you walk along the road, when you lie down and when you get up. Tie them as symbols on your hands and bind them on your foreheads. Write them on the doorframes of your houses and on your gates."
—Deuteronomy 6:4-9

E-COURAGEMENT BLAST 2

Each of these E-couragement Blasts is included on the CD-ROM, in both rich text format (RTF) and portable document file (PDF). Feel free to edit these e-couragements to match your ministry and the needs of your volunteers.

Listen

Brain Food

Everyone loves it when others are interested in him or her. Not everyone is looking to be the center of attention, but we all crave acceptance and relationships. We all want to be known. Questions provide a great way to know others, so one of your jobs as a youth worker is to ask questions.

Ask. Wait. Listen. Watch. Ask again.

I want to challenge you to become an expert about your students. The only way to become an expert is to ask good questions so you can know your material inside and out. Ask personal questions, questions that cause your students to think, open up, and share what really matters to them. Ask questions that challenge them and help them see where God is working in their life.

Ask and listen. Don't give students all the answers. Don't talk forever about yourself. Students hear enough lectures and probably don't need another one. Listening shows you care and builds trust—which can lead to a relationship that impacts them for an eternity.

Like They Say...

"Learning to ask good questions opens relational doors, deepens the possibility for fellowship, and sets the stage for personal growth. Start asking!"
—Steve Merritt, *Group Magazine*

God's Word

"Once when Jesus was praying in private and his disciples were with him, he asked them, 'Who do the crowds say I am?'

"They replied, 'Some say John the Baptist; others say Elijah; and still others, that one of the prophets of long ago has come back to life.'

" 'But what about you?' he asked. 'Who do you say I am?'

"Peter answered, 'The Christ of God.' "—Luke 9:18-20

E-COURAGEMENT BLAST 3

Each of these E-couragement Blasts is included on the CD-ROM, in both rich text format (RTF) and portable document file (PDF). Feel free to edit these e-couragements to match your ministry and the needs of your volunteers.

Investment

Brain Food

You probably wouldn't be involved with youth ministry if you didn't also enjoy hanging out with teenagers and building relationships. Way to go! It's easy, however, to focus on the students with whom you share a similar sense of humor or a common interest. God made people different, and tapping into those niche areas is great for ministry. It's okay that you don't know every student in your ministry if there are other adults investing in their lives. Focus on building deep and lasting relationships with the students whom God has given you in your small group, on a retreat, or wherever you may be.

Nonetheless, sometimes it takes a little more effort. If you're stuck in a place where you can't connect with anyone or are the only person on your ministry team, that's okay! Three cheers for your commitment! Keep asking students their names. Keep asking them questions and getting to know them. Show up at a game, play, concert, or where a student works. It'll show that you truly do desire to get to know their world, not only as someone who asks about it but also as a participant. You'll begin to develop life-changing and lasting friendships.

Make sure to also target those students who might be on the fringe, those who don't seem connected to the ministry or other adults. They probably act as if they don't care, but a friendship initiated by you is probably what they're screaming for in their heart.

Like They Say…

"A knight on a journey who was seeking the King and picked the Prince as his traveling companion said, 'There is no one else I would have trusted…As we journeyed, he played your song. I learned it so well that though a thousand false flutes tried to hide your music, I could hear your song above them all. It was with me all the way.'"

—Max Lucado, *With You All the Way*

God's Word

"I pray that you may be active in sharing your faith, so that you will have a full understanding of every good thing we have in Christ."—Philemon 6

E-COURAGEMENT BLAST 4

Each of these E-couragement Blasts is included on the CD-ROM, in both rich text format (RTF) and portable document file (PDF). Feel free to edit these e-couragements to match your ministry and the needs of your volunteers.

Relationships That Matter

Brain Food

Who is in the stands cheering for you in the marathon of life?

We've all had people in our past who believed in us when we didn't have the strength to believe in ourselves. Being a youth worker means that you get the privilege of doing this for someone else. So keep up the good work. Keep encouraging. Continue to remember names. And dive deep into the lives of the students you are walking through life with.

A teenager's life includes his or her family. Even though parents might sometimes be the scariest people in youth ministry, get to know them as well. Not only will connecting with parents show the student how much you care, but as parents get to know you, they will give you more and more trust and freedom to hang out with and mentor their son or daughter.

Like They Say...

"The Christian leader is called to help others affirm this great news, and to make visible in daily events the fact that behind the dirty curtain of our painful symptoms there is something great to be seen: the face of Him in whose image we were shaped."—Henri J. M. Nouwen, *The Wounded Healer: Ministry in Contemporary Society*

God's Word

"All over the world this gospel is bearing fruit and growing, just as it has been doing among you since the day you heard it and understood God's grace in all its truth."—Colossians 1:6

E-COURAGEMENT BLAST 5

Each of these E-couragement Blasts is included on the CD-ROM, in both rich text format (RTF) and portable document file (PDF). Feel free to edit these e-couragements to match your ministry and the needs of your volunteers.

Fill Your Brain

Brain Food

Solomon had the chance to ask God for anything. Think about that for a moment. Any of his wildest dreams would be granted. He didn't ask for riches or that people would like him. Instead, he asked for wisdom. Just wisdom.

Solomon set a great example for all leaders. Being teachable is an invaluable quality in youth ministry, and it's important to start early. Don't get overwhelmed by trying to read every book on youth ministry when you first start out—there are tons of books, Web sites, magazines, and conferences—but do try to keep up with some of the resources available. Ask others in ministry what they're reading and what they've learned lately.

Strange as it may seem, one of the best, yet most often overlooked, resources to learn from is parents. Yes, parents. It's easy to ignore them and only call when you need a driver or someone to bring snacks. But remember, they know and love their teenagers more than you ever will. Partnering with them will not only show them how much you care about their family but also help their teenager grow in his or her relationship with Jesus.

Like They Say...

"If we cannot be His students, we have no way to learn to exist always and everywhere within the riches and power of His Word."—J. P. Moreland, *Love Your God With All Your Mind: The Role of Reason in the Life of the Soul*

God's Word

"Don't turn your back on wisdom, for she will protect you. Love her, and she will guard you."

—Proverbs 4:6, New Living Translation

E-COURAGEMENT BLAST 6

Each of these E-couragement Blasts is included on the CD-ROM, in both rich text format (RTF) and portable document file (PDF). Feel free to edit these e-couragements to match your ministry and the needs of your volunteers.

Ministry Is Messy

Brain Food

Relationships are messy. One person offends another. Someone gets annoyed. Imperfect people ruin our perfect plans.

Conflict happens. That's expected.

What's often unexpected, sadly, is appropriate handling of the conflict. When people come to you to talk about situations that bother them, they mostly want to be heard. It's important to listen and acknowledge their feelings.

The same is probably true for you. When a situation is frustrating, it's easy to vent.

But let's be honest. Venting can often mean gossiping about a person or a situation from a limited perspective, which does nothing to help the actual problem—and definitely doesn't honor God.

Instead of immediately venting, take a minute to breathe deeply and seek God's wisdom. Then approach the situation in a way that follows Scripture and respects others, even if it's the toughest option.

Keep up the good but hard work of setting an example for the teenagers in your ministry.

Like They Say...

"When through the blood of the everlasting covenant we children of the shadows reach at last our home in the light, we shall have a thousand strings to our harps, but the sweetest may well be the one tuned to sound forth most perfectly the mercy of God."—A. W. Tozer, *The Knowledge of the Holy*

God's Word

"Bless those who persecute you; bless and do not curse. Rejoice with those who rejoice; mourn with those who mourn. Live in harmony with one another. Do not be proud, but be willing to associate with people of low position. Do not be conceited. Do not repay anyone evil for evil. Be careful to do what is right in the eyes of everybody. If it is possible, as far as it depends on you, live at peace with everyone."
—Romans 12:14-18

E-COURAGEMENT BLAST 7

Each of these E-couragement Blasts is included on the CD-ROM, in both rich text format (RTF) and portable document file (PDF). Feel free to edit these e-couragements to match your ministry and the needs of your volunteers.

Lead First

Brain Food

Raise the bar high, and your students will reach for it. Typically, when students are given the chance, they will act responsibly.

However, sometimes teenagers will be teenagers. Something will happen that merits reponse, and when you ask what they were thinking, you might find out that they weren't—thinking, that is.

Don't be afraid to discipline appropriately. Remember, you are called to be their youth leader. Be confident in the discipline part of this role in discipleship. Those words go hand in hand, and God is using you to mold students into his disciples.

Like They Say...

"From our own struggles, God intends to lead us into deeper life in Him. And beyond our personal need to find our own way in spirit, we are being trained so that we can later lead others who wish to grow in a strong, living faith."—Howard Baker, *Soul Keeping: Ancient Paths of Spiritual Direction*

God's Word

"Come, let us return to the Lord. He has torn us to pieces but he will heal us; he has injured us but he will bind up our wounds."—Hosea 6:1

E-COURAGEMENT BLAST 8

Each of these E-couragement Blasts is included on the CD-ROM, in both rich text format (RTF) and portable document file (PDF). Feel free to edit these e-couragements to match your ministry and the needs of your volunteers.

Tending the Flock

Brain Food

As a career, shepherding would probably be pretty foreign to most youth workers if it weren't in the Bible. It may be an outdated profession, but it's still a job that can teach us about ministry.

Shepherds don't just kind of recognize their sheep at the mall. They don't simply wonder about that face showing up to Bible study. They know the names of their sheep. They acknowledge each individual sheep's role and significance in the flock.

Shepherds also don't leave their sheep in the same place. Once the grass is eaten in one area, shepherds bring them to new ground, making sure there is time for rest and sources of water.

Continue to guide your students at a pace that helps your students discover who God made them to be. It's a process that takes time and intentionality; thank you for going through it as you shepherd teenagers.

Like They Say…

"Being a spiritual director is bringing the same care and skill and intensity to the ordinary, boring, uneventful parts of our lives that we readily give to the eventful conversions and proclamations."—Eugene H. Peterson, *Working the Angles: The Shape of Pastoral Integrity*

God's Word

"What do you think? If a man owns a hundred sheep, and one of them wanders away, will he not leave the ninety-nine on the hills and go to look for the one that wandered off? And if he finds it, I tell you the truth, he is happier about that one sheep than about the ninety-nine that did not wander off. In the same way your Father in heaven is not willing that any of these little ones should be lost."
—Matthew 18:12-14

E-COURAGEMENT BLAST 9

Each of these E-couragement Blasts is included on the CD-ROM, in both rich text format (RTF) and portable document file (PDF). Feel free to edit these e-couragements to match your ministry and the needs of your volunteers.

They Left You in Charge...Now What?

Brain Food

At first, the thought of being a small-group leader doesn't sound scary, and you agree to do it. Then, the more you think about it, the scarier it gets. Facing a small group of students, possibly alone, and being responsible for leading discussion, building relationships, and having fun together—that's a big responsibility.

All of a sudden, you're trying to think of a good excuse to get out of your commitment.

Is that how you felt the first time you led a small group of students? Or you might have been so excited that you weren't a bit nervous. You might not even think much at all about leading a small group because it's become old habit.

If so, that's great! It reflects the comfort and confidence you have in the relationships you've built and in your calling to minister to students.

Nonetheless, even the most seasoned youth workers take time to focus on how they can be more intentional about helping students discover more about God, the Bible, life, and themselves; reviewing the basics; remembering healthy boundaries; asking good questions; listening to students more; and evaluating each small group meeting.

Don't give up, and don't stop having fun.

Like They Say...

"Knowing God's heart means consistently, radically, and very concretely to announce and reveal that God is love and only love, and that every time fear, isolation, or despair begins to invade the human soul, this is not something that comes from God."—Henri J. M. Nouwen, *In the Name of Jesus: Reflections on Christian Leadership*

God's Word

"For God did not give us a spirit of timidity, but a spirit of power, of love, and of self-discipline."—2 Timothy 1:7

E-COURAGEMENT BLAST 10

Each of these E-couragement Blasts is included on the CD-ROM, in both rich text format (RTF) and portable document file (PDF). Feel free to edit these e-couragements to match your ministry and the needs of your volunteers.

Love God—Enough Said

Brain Food

Love God. Even though he'll always love you more than you could ever love him back, love God. Love God with everything in you. Chew on that. Focus on that. Do things that grow this love. Pray about it.

No matter how great a youth leader you try to be, you're useless without love for God. Focusing on loving God is what God calls you to do, and that calling trumps your role in youth ministry.

Who you are should determine what you do, not the other way around. Look at your life—is it a reflection of your love for God? Is it a growing love that runs deep?

Take time to rest in the Lord. It's okay to choose rest over ministry sometimes. Be with God. Focus on your relationship with him. It's not selfish. It's healthy and will fill you up to go out and be an even more effective youth leader than you already are.

Like They Say...

"Sociologists have a theory of the looking-glass self: you become what the most important person in your life…thinks you are. How would my life change if I truly believed the Bible's astounding words about God's love for me, if I looked in the mirror and saw what God sees?"—Philip D. Yancey, *What's So Amazing About Grace?*

God's Word

"Because of the Lord's great love we are not consumed, for his compassions never fail. They are new every morning; great is your faithfulness. I say to myself, 'The Lord is my portion; therefore I will wait for him.' "—Lamentations 3:22-24

E-COURAGEMENT BLAST 11

Each of these E-couragement Blasts is included on the CD-ROM, in both rich text format (RTF) and portable document file (PDF). Feel free to edit these e-couragements to match your ministry and the needs of your volunteers.

You're Not Alone

Brain Food

Batman had Robin. Seinfeld hung out with George. Monica, Rachel, Phoebe, Chandler, Ross, and Joey gathered in Central Perk as friends. Michael Jordan played with the Chicago Bulls. Moses partnered with Aaron. And Paul took Barnabas along. Good things come from teams.

God did not design us to live life alone. Eve was created to be in relationship and work with Adam. Jesus picked his team—the 12 disciples.

Jesus taught us the most about teamwork. He was the coach and asked his players to cooperate, even when they were confused, frustrated, and tired, in order to focus on his mission.

Sometimes, ministry is the same way. Your lead youth worker is not Jesus, but this person does shoulder great responsibility.

Thanks for partnering with others to help teenagers grow in their relationship with Jesus.

Like They Say…

"Discipleship is a team effort. He asks us to be disciples so that we might make disciples."—Mark Bailey, *To Follow Him: The Seven Marks of a Disciple*

God's Word

"Glorify the Lord with me; let us exalt his name together."—Psalm 34:3

E-COURAGEMENT BLAST 12

Each of these E-couragement Blasts is included on the CD-ROM, in both rich text format (RTF) and portable document file (PDF). Feel free to edit these e-couragements to match your ministry and the needs of your volunteers.

Speak Intentionally

Brain Food

Words are a powerful tool in ministry. They're like dandelion seeds blowing in the wind. Once your words are out there, there's no pulling them back.

As a youth worker, you can use this double-edged sword to build up students, speak truth, comfort where there is hurt, and challenge teenagers to grow spiritually.

It's no mistake that James 3 teaches us to be intentional about the power of the tongue. It's a dynamic muscle with great potential. Continue to flex it in ways that bring God glory and encourage students!

Like They Say...

"Kind words can be short and easy to speak, but their echoes are truly endless."
—Mother Teresa

God's Word

"Do not let any unwholesome talk come out of your mouths, but only what is helpful for building others up according to their needs, that it may benefit those who listen."—Ephesians 4:29

Pass It On Conference on DVD
Valuable youth ministry training with Doug Fields & Jim Burns

Learn it. Own it. Teach it. What you receive...Pass It On!

Pass It On
Youth Ministry Nuts & Bolts DVD Set
Valuable DVD training for building a healthy youth ministry foundation

This installment of the Pass It On conference covers the steps necessary to recruit, train, and empower volunteers and student leaders. It's an entire weekend conference worth of sessions, handouts, PowerPoint slides and notes to help get the most from your volunteers

Pass It On
Helping Hurting Kids DVD Set
Valuable DVD training for working with hurting kids

We know you want to help your students who are in pain, so get the resources to minister to students and teach others. We've included teaching notes, PowerPoint presentations, participant guides, and a video of the conference too (of course)!

simplyyouthministry.com
simplifying ministry...saving you time

toll free: 1-866-9-simply
simplyyouthministry.com

Visit simplyyouthministry.com to find more volunteer training resources

Mentor Me Year 1
12 reproducible volunteer training sessions on CD

Whether you have one volunteer or one hundred, you know how important they are to the success of your ministry. Give them incredible tools crafted by some of the brightest minds in youth ministry, and you won't believe the impact they'll have. This collection of 12 reproducible sessions, each under one hour, are a powerful tool to help you develop your volunteer staff.

Leaders are Learners
Ten 15-minute volunteer training sessions on CD

You have a small army of willing volunteers. How do you equip them to effectively minister to students? Get your entire volunteer team on the same page with these reproducible audio training sessions.

This resource isn't designed to replace an all-day seminar or a good youth ministry book, but it encourages and trains leaders with bite-size chunks of leadership training.

simplifying ministry...saving you time

toll free: 1-866-9-simply
simplyyouthministry.com